Praise for Reclaiming Your Energy from Your Emotions:

Dr. Lammers makes clear the processes by which our personal energy has become stuck, together with energy from others, to produce the various painful and limiting emotions and beliefs which hamper us. He shares his discovery that using words — three sentences, accurately focused — releases the stuck energy and frees us, free to be who we truly are, and to accomplish what we truly intend.

Dr. Nancy Porter-Steele, Ph.D., MFT, TSTA

Dr. Lammers outlines how the use of Logosynthesis will assist the reader to reclaim ownership and connection regarding life and living in more healthy thinking and feeling states.

John H. Diepold, Jr., Ph.D.
Originator, Developer, and Author of Heart
Assisted Therapy® (HAT®)

Willem takes us skillfully through the gamut of emotions we as human beings feel. He explains how our interactions with others can trigger these emotions, and then shows us how we, as professionals, can work with our clients to alleviate their distress and restore the flow of energy.

Mary O'Donoghue, MNAPCP, MEASC, SAI
CEO Logosynthesis® Academy

This book is a collection of essays on human experience, cataloging familiar binds that entangle us in daily life. Through his deep experience as a psychologist, counselor, and wise openhearted human, Dr. Lammers fits the puzzle pieces of life together that are universally shared by humanity using a process that isas personal and tender as our heartbeat when we suffer.

Lori Chortkoff Hops, Ph.D., DCEP
Licensed Psychologist
President-Elect for ACEP (2020)

RECLAIMING YOUR ENERGY FROM YOUR EMOTIONS

STATES OF THE MIND IN LOGOSYNTHESIS®

SEE YOUR SELF, BE YOUR SELF

DR. WILLEM LAMMERS

WITH LARA CARDONA MORISSET

THE ORIGIN OF
LOGOSYNTHESIS®

The Origin of Logosynthesis®

Bristol House, Bahnhofstrasse 38, 7310 Bad Ragaz, Switzerland.

www.logosynthesis.net, info@logosynthesis.net

1st edition, 2020, Version 27.03.2020

ISBN: 978-1077348783

Cover design and typesetting: Ian Dennis

This book is available in print from most online retailers.

TABLE OF CONTENTS

TABLE OF CONTENTS

Logosynthesis can disrupt your patterns. Resolving the frozen worlds associated with your emotional experience leads to a state of astonishing stillness and quiet. In the beginning, you become concerned because you no longer recognize your old self in this new world. You stay calm in traffic, listen to your critics with interest rather than defensiveness, and smile while gently saying no. All these situations used to generate intense, overwhelming, emotional reactions. You considered these emotions part of your identity.

At first, life seems empty now, until you begin to discover the small changes. You're greeted spontaneously by people on the street. At work, people seem more friendly and cooperative. You're told you look great or asked if you've been away. You suddenly sign up for a course you've long wanted to attend, and your love life blossoms like a cherry tree in spring. At some point, you even forget to buy cigarettes. You suddenly notice you're finishing things in time instead of procrastinating.

You are here, living your destiny, and it doesn't even need to look like a big thing.

Logosynthesis is a wonderful instrument with which to address the negative emotions and limiting beliefs addressed in this book.

There are less and less people who read a book from cover to cover nowadays. Therefore, I've chosen to write this book in a way that fits several reading styles:

- You can start at the beginning and read until the end. In this case you will notice that the content of the chapters follows a line from deeply negative emotions through more or less neutral to the highly positive energy of love and bliss.

- You can choose to explore negative emotions, bound in frozen energy, in part I, or you can focus on positive emotions, resulting from freely flowing energy, in part II.

- You can just open it, start to read and let your Self be inspired by the page in front of you.

This book assumes basic knowledge about Logosynthesis. It is a compilation of essays I posted on the Logosynthesis Facebook group between 2013 and 2019. They have been edited to make them accessible for a larger group of readers, but you will gain the most if you have a background in the worldview, the attitude, the theory and the methods of Logosynthesis.

If you're not yet familiar with the technique, I invite you to read the description of the technique on page 129 in the appendix. The appendix also contains a glossary of terms that will help you to follow the theory behind the themes in each chapter.

If you want to know more, there are several options:

- You can join the Logosynthesis Facebook group or another group in your own language: Logosynthese, Logosintesi, Logosynthèse, etc.

- Laurie Weiss' little book *Letting It Go* shows how to start using Logosynthesis in daily life.

- My book *Self-Coaching with Logosynthesis* offers an introduction to using the model for yourself at a deeper level.

- If you're a professional in counseling, coaching or psychotherapy and you want to use Logosynthesis in your work, I recommend you to read *Logosynthesis—A Handbook for the Helping Professions, with a preface by Dr. Fred Gallo.*

- My book *Minute Miracles: The Practice of Logosynthesis* contains a series of concrete examples of the application of Logosynthesis in my consulting room.

These books are available from most online retailers.

You will notice that this book addresses *you* many times. This is intentional: you're invited to explore whether this concept or situation applies to you as a person. If you don't relate to what I'm describing, it's an opportunity to identify with the reality of other people: your friends or family, or if you're a professional in the field, your clients.

In my practice as a coach and a psychotherapist the latter strategy has often helped me to make contact with clients I didn't understand or feel comfortable with at first. Standing in their shoes also made it easier to find the right intervention in that moment of the process.

Working with Logosynthesis requires a precise tuning into the field of another person. You're offering an open space in which your client can be present with everything that's moving or freezing them. You keep holding that space during the entire process, without judgment or a hidden agenda. From there you can carefully assist your client in discovering, activating and neutralizing those memories, fantasies and beliefs that stand in the way of a better life.

I want to thank Lara Cardona Morisset for her great help in compiling a wealth of Facebook posts into one coherent text, Ian Dennis for his design of the cover and the typesetting, Kris Ferraro for her precise way of editing, as well as Karla Marie Dawe, Raya Williams and Satinder Bhalla for their fantastic help in the last stage of the publication process.

I feel deeply grateful to all those who have helped me to formulate questions and answers, especially the members of our Logosynthesis community in our Facebook groups. They have supported and challenged me over the years in lively and fruitful interactions.

Bad Ragaz, at the foot of the Swiss Alps,
in the first month of the corona crisis 2020,

Dr. Willem Lammers

Giving up the idea that someone else can make you feel a certain way is *mighty* difficult. We are all well-versed in causality. It's natural to see A then B happen in short order and draw a cause-effect relationship between the two. Simple reasoning tells us that if we see a dirty dish in the sink and feel angry, then the dish in the sink has made us angry, and the blame lies with the one who put it there. There is a light-speed stimulus-response pattern between the sight of it and a feeling of being disrespected.

As you practice using Logosynthesis as your first response rather than confronting the dish-in-sink-leaver directly, a flaw in your thinking appears: If you knew this familiar feeling long before you met your current kitchen partner, when you were 20, and 10, and perhaps even 5: How can they be the cause? There's a connection, yes, but not causality.

The real magic begins when you spend some time applying Logosynthesis, for yourself or with a trained professional, addressing these earlier experiences. Then one day you notice you're looking at a sink piled high with dirty dishes and you feel fine. You leave them there, ask their maker to clean them, or you clean them yourself for the sake of a clean kitchen. New options are available to you because you will have the freedom of choosing your reaction. You've broken the dish rage cycle—not the dish.

YOU'VE GOTTA DANCE LIKE
THERE'S NOBODY WATCHING...

You've gotta dance like there's nobody watching,
Love like you'll never be hurt,
Sing like there's nobody listening,
And live like it's heaven on earth.

— William W. Purkey

Your emotions may be yours, but you are not your emotions. The belief that *You Make Me Feel* is one of the most popular and widespread blocks to personal and spiritual growth. The question is not whether emotions are negative or positive. The problem is the belief that the behavior of someone else causes you to feel a certain way—automatically. Sooner or later this erroneous belief will cause you trouble.

A belief is the assumption that two things are connected. Sometimes there is no doubt about it: If you drop an apple, it will fall on the ground. If you pay your bills, you'll stay in the black. When these beliefs follow a set of experiences all human beings share, then they're called facts. Other beliefs are not so matter of fact, as any political discussion will quickly reveal.

If you believe that *You Make Me Feel*, that belief will take away your power. You become dependent on what others are showing, saying and doing. If your neighbor, colleague or friend gets angry at you, tells you that you're wrong, you'll probably react. However, you're the one responsible for the quality of that reaction: If you respect their anger and listen patiently to their grudges, if you show anger too, or if you feel ashamed, guilty or sad.

Once you start to explore *You Make Me Feel* instead of assuming it's a fact, you're in for an interesting journey. You will discover this belief wherever you look and listen, and you'll probably also find it within yourself. Once you've understood the mechanism of how the belief works, it may be pretty confronting to discover it in yourself and to notice how often it happens.

What happens in *You Make Me Feel*?

A behavior—a movement, a sentence, a facial expression—leads to automatic reactions in another person. These reactions follow the behavior immediately, covering a whole gamut of emotions: guilt, shame, fear, sadness, anger, joy and pride. The person who reacts is firmly convinced that the other "caused" it, whereby the emotions can be negative or positive. Your colleague can make you feel powerless and anxious by bullying you, or you can feel joyful if you receive a diamond ring from your lover. *You Make Me Feel* can be confirmed from both sides.

If your relationships with others are based on mutual respect, it makes sense to explore the dynamics of *You Make Me Feel* for all involved. The stable base of the relationship will help both of you overcome the limitations of a *You Make Me Feel* assumption.

If there is a lack of trust and respect in your relationships, you're either a victim of physical and emotional abuse, or you're abusive yourself. Such patterns often have a long history and don't change easily. You may need help from friends, relatives, a life coach or a psychotherapist. The way out of the destructive pattern may begin with these questions:

- *Which behavior of the other is disturbing you most in this relationship?*

- *How do you feel when they behave like this?*
- *What do you believe about yourself in this situation?*
- *What do you believe about the other person?*
- *What do you believe about your world?*
- *What would shift if you changed those beliefs?*

and finally:

- *Do you know these behaviors and reactions from an earlier period in your life?*

From my experience as a guide to people in trouble, I guess that your reactions have been a part of your life for a long time, and that the person you're living or working with now is the latest in a long line of people to whom you've reacted to in a similar way. This book may help you to recognize new aspects of such patterns and to find ways to resolve it. If you are unable to change the situation on your own, ask for help from people you know you can trust: friends, family, a minister, life coach, counselor, or psychotherapist.

If you assume that another person is responsible for the fulfillment of your needs or desires, a *You Make Me Feel* assumption leads to problems: The other person should make you happy, take care of you, and keep you happy. In today's consumer society, many people have learned to expect to have their needs fulfilled, and these expectations have slowly filtered into people's thinking about relationships, leading to higher and higher expectations. A partner must be pretty, smart, sexy, slim, sensitive, as well as understanding and available, and above all a good cook, cleaner and gardener. In other words: as perfect as life on Instagram. A *You Make Me*

Feel connection between these expectations and the reality of a fallible human being will trigger negative emotions: shame, guilt, anger, disappointment, frustration, sadness or a fear of abandonment.

Since these emotions are closely associated with the presence, or in the case of abandonment issues, the absence of the partner, people have a deep, irrational tendency to attribute the cause of their feelings to their partner. Then *You Make Me Feel* becomes active. The emotions can easily start a crisis or conflict in the relationship: It's connected to the belief that the other should not make you feel this way.

You have worked all day, your colleagues behaved terribly, your boss expected far too much. When you arrive home, you expect at least one person is willing to listen to your sad story. However, your partner's day wasn't much better. Your oldest kid has been acting rebelliously all day and the younger one had a fight with a friend. Both partners expect to be seen and to be heard, but chances are that you both won't get what you need, especially if you believe in *You Make Me Feel*. Many people are only willing to meet another's needs after they themselves have felt seen and heard.

If you recognize yourself in this description of *You Make Me Feel*, the best treatment is to identify the fantasy worlds behind the expectations and to dissolve them with the help of the Logosynthesis sentences. This will help you to reconnect to the present and allow you to make an adult assessment of your situation:

- *Is it realistic to expect this given the present situation?*

- *Does the other person need something from me as well?*
- *Does it make sense to let the other person's needs come first?*

If you address and treat the belief *You Make Me Feel* numerous times under various circumstances, you will note that your own needs become less dominant in the partnership. You will reduce the mutually generated stress and paradoxically, you might get more of your needs met than ever before.

Many people grew up in an environment that didn't fulfill their needs. Their parents acted irrationally or emotionally. If your parents rejected or denied your needs as a child, and you hold them responsible for this, you can become locked in a pattern of frozen reactions to these painful memories of your parents. This not only poisons your relationships, but through transference mechanisms, will also limit others in meeting you.

An interesting question: Where do these emotions of the parents come from? They were born as curious, loving babies eager to learn and develop. Their own parents were born the same, but what made your parents and grandparents react in this way?

There may be a political system, a religion, a war, the culture of a village, a city or a country, which still runs through the veins of the child that became your parent.

The more you explore the above patterns, the clearer it will become to you that the needs you want others to fulfill are the same ones your parents did not respond to when you were a child. Then it's time to resolve the distressing memories of having been ignored, neglected, rejected, or left alone.

The Logosynthesis sentences can help you to neutralize such memories: on your own or with the help of a trained professional.

Then you'll notice that you've become an adult and realize that you're able to take care of yourself now. You've become sadder—and wiser. The first stage of growing is growing up.

MOVING INWARD:
ENERGY BOUND IN SUFFERING

DESPAIR:
THE BLACK HOLE

If a baby's needs for love and care are not fulfilled, people land in what Logosynthesis calls the *black hole*. In this state you feel utterly lonely and miserable, without awareness of your Divine origin, and without feeling connected to other human beings. You don't see how to escape the black hole. Some lives begin in this emotional state. People entered this plane with a body and a mind that needed love, support and compassion in every single moment, and the parents they met in this world were not able to fulfill these needs, for various reasons:

- The parents didn't know how to fulfill the needs of the child, because their own childhood needs hadn't been fulfilled.

- They weren't ready to have a child.

- They didn't want any more children.

- Their bodies and minds were occupied with their own plans, or with the struggle to make ends meet.

- They were physically or mentally exhausted and didn't have the energy for a child.

In short, the parents couldn't be present. As a result, the child went into a frozen state, disconnected from Essence, and also disconnected from their parents. This is such a painful state that any child will do anything to avoid it, and since a newborn is extremely creative, they will accept all available options.

If a part of your life energy is stuck in this black hole, you'll try anything to avoid this deepest form of loneliness and despair. Your first option is to look for stability, for structure. In the aftermath of a traumatic transition into this life, you tend to find stability in thoughts, feelings and convictions that *you are not OK*. You start to believe that something is wrong with you. In the Logosynthesis model, this is called first order dissociation. Because this preverbal conclusion hurts deeply, you'll try and find all kinds of ways to escape it.

This set of solutions to avoid the pain and get basic needs met is the field of second order dissociation in Logosynthesis. As long as you stay in this field you can manage to repress the pain and stabilize your basic position. Your being OK becomes subject to conditions:

- *I'm OK when I'm working hard.*

- *I'm OK when I'm the best at something.*

- *I'm OK when everyone likes me.*

- *I'm OK when I'm helping others.*

- *I'm OK when people show me respect.*

- *I'm OK when I'm in control of the situation.*

- *I'm OK when I'm eating.*

- *I'm OK when I'm high or drunk.*

In time, the ways you have discovered to feel OK, your second order dissociation patterns, will have disadvantages: This is what we call third order dissociation. If you're the greatest, your position will be constantly under attack, if you're an addict it may ruin your life, and if you're overworking, you may burn out. Your original solution for being OK then becomes a new problem.

In all types of dissociated states, we see a strong attachment to patterns and structures. People's life energy is bound in these patterns: you could say they're addicted to them. Some people cannot see that there is more to life than rigid patterns. They cannot imagine a world without preset ways to feel, think and act, other than the total panic of the *black hole*. That's why people tend to stay in a situation that's familiar. A wife stays with an abusive husband, because the world is familiar that way. A man lives in a violent neighborhood because his friends live there. Many people hate their jobs, but the fear of the unknown keeps them at their workplace until retirement. The familiar offers a feeling of safety, even if it hurts.

Letting go of such limiting structures will always activate past pain. Normally, childhood trauma and abandonment will pick up the disguise of problems in the present, and those who enter therapy or counseling may not be aware of this mechanism. They are only aware of the problems of their present world, but these are often metaphors for traumas from childhood, or earlier, at birth or even conception. If people have experienced traumatic events in these intense transitions this will influence the way they engage with the world during their whole life.

Conception, birth and early childhood can bring major shocks for a being that enters a human body and mind. The parents are not ready to conceive a child, and the circumstances are not welcoming: There is no love, perhaps even abuse and violence. Working your way through these shocks can be part of the process you have to go through.

If much of your energy is bound in such a black hole, the only way to bring light into it is finding a safe place with a counselor or a psychotherapist who can meet you in this loneliness and despair. Only when people feel safe with another human being can they start to look beyond the familiar, they can learn to see that it's not really a black hole: It's just a part that has been split off and frozen in the moment they lost their awareness of Essence. That happens in moments of unbearable pain and suffering—for body and mind.

The most elegant way I know to reconnect to Essence through the black hole is through the application of Logosynthesis. In the safe space of the group or the consultancy room you can start to explore the moment you entered this world. You will discover that you survived those intense, painful moments and grew through them. There is nothing to be afraid of anymore.

You will find more on the black hole and the conception shock in the next book of this series, *Sparks at Dawn. Awakening with Logosynthesis.*

If you are disconnected from Essence as well as from other people, you experience loneliness and abandonment. In its extreme form, you re-experience the black hole described above, briefly or for an extended period. When you entered the world of form, you were confronted with the pains of the body and the limitations of the mind. The awareness of your innate power and immortality was left behind.

In loneliness you are aware of a need to connect, to belong, to be part of a community. You're not aware of the fact that you are Essence, part of an infinitely larger Whole, the creative principle of the Universe.

Solitude is different. In solitude, you are enough, your Self is enough, you are whole. You don't need constant attention and affection, you don't need others to validate what you do or what you are, and others cannot count upon your validation. Endless superficial conversations become annoying: You don't need to talk anymore to fill your time. You are here, but you don't need to constantly prove yourself. For those around you, this can be uncomfortable, as if you're breaking the rules. You' don't play the game of mutual confirmation, and others may consider you aloof or arrogant. In reality, you just didn't have anything to say.

Solitude is a side effect of the ongoing practice of Logosynthesis. At first, it will feel horrible, and you won't be able to tell it apart from loneliness. On the surface it looks the same: You don't feel attached or attracted to patterns of mutual satisfaction anymore. In the Logosynthesis model, the logical consequence of this is the reactivation of early experiences of disconnection and abandonment from others. Once you have processed these with the help of the sentences and with a guide who's been there and knows what you're going through, you start reconnecting to Essence and discover that you don't need to rely on those connections anymore. The awareness of Essence shortcuts these psychological needs.

From this awareness, a brand-new attitude towards people and the world develops. Once you've reconnected with Essence, love and compassion begin to grow, not as negotiated forms of exchange, but as a continuous flow from Essence, through you and into the world.

Solitude in connection with Essence can become a continuous source of love and affection for those around you, in a way that resolves their patterns, opening other hearts to the flow. Loneliness is a deficit. Solitude is a resource: It carries the energy of Essence.

HOMESICKNESS,
LOVESICKNESS

*The good enough mother meets the omnipotent child
and, to an extent, makes sense of it.*

— Donald Winnicott

Years ago, Dianne Connolly wrote a wise and poetic book called *All Sickness is Home Sickness*. In our terms, that title means that in every one of us there is a deep longing to be reconnected to our ultimate Home: Essence. It means that there is an awareness beyond words that something is missing in the world you're living in, even though at the surface everything seems perfect.

The word *home* contains two aspects: There is an awareness of your true core, and at the same time you're aware of Essence in those around you. That's why the difference between a house and a home is very clear: A house is an object, a piece of real estate. A home is alive with smiles, voices, music and hugs, and to feel that the home is alive with the energy of those you love, you must be aware of Essence, the Love in your Self.

If such a home isn't there, sickness is one way to connect to the people around you, even though it's limiting, crippling. In seeing clients with physical symptoms, I often notice a disconnection between their way of being and what they really are: They don't know their purpose in life, and it depends on others if they feel good or bad. Often, they turn to driver behavior in order to be respected or loved. They're doing their best, they're in a hurry, trying to be strong or to please others.

After they have been doing that for a long time, their bodies start giving signals that something is wrong. This is done in a language that cannot be understood by a conscious mind occupied by the obligations set by the world around them in return for love and affection.

The disconnection has a long history most of the time. It dates back to when the person entered existence, when they had very limited means to tell their environment what was going on in them. The parents were occupied by their own sorrow or anger and unable to recognize the divine character of their child. In Donald Winnicott's words, they couldn't make sense of its needs to be seen, heard, and held.

If these needs are not met, the child risks losing the sense of home. Its physical and emotional signals are not read, and then the child will stop giving those signals. The free energy that was available to connect with the environment is locked into patterns of the young body and the unprogrammed mind. That energy will stay frozen until the adult person discovers that something is missing and starts the journey of retrieving the frozen energy bound in the limiting patterns.

The same could be said for lovesickness, for Essence is Love. As a matter of fact, we get sick when we're driven by the needs of body and mind, and only the reconnection with Essence will heal us, make us whole.

Homesickness or lovesickness in the usual sense means that we believe that we need a place or a person to make us happy. However, focusing on the satisfaction of needs may keep us disconnected from what we really are.

A place or a person can make us feel at home. A beloved person can open a window to the Divine, but if we mistake this experience as resulting from a quality of that person, we ignore our deepest Self. In fact, it takes the Divine in your Self to recognize the Divine in the other.

HELPLESS

Helpless, helpless, helpless, helpless
Babe, can you hear me now?
The chains are locked and tied across the door
Baby, sing with me somehow.

— Neil Young
from the album Crosby, Stills, Nash, and Young

If you feel helpless, you're alone in a world without support. You feel bad and don't see a way out: *The chains are locked and tied across the door.* Loneliness is the worst, and that's why the singer calls on his babe to sing with him.

You're frozen in this state, overwhelmed by emotions, without rational thinking, and without taking action to change your situation. If you're feeling helpless, you're holding onto several beliefs that confirm and reinforce each other:

1. *I'm in a situation that makes me feel miserable.*

2. *That situation must be changed.*

3. *I cannot change my own life. I'm helpless. I'm alone.*

4. *Someone must change my situation: Everyone else is less miserable than I am. They are able to run their work and life well and have great relationships. I need those people to tell me how I should change.*

5. *If I meet someone, I assume this person is able to help me, because they are more powerful than I am.*

6. *If I share my sad life story with them, they can change my situation for me.*

If the people in belief #6 don't change your situation, you return to belief #1. To break this chain, identify and address any of these beliefs with the Logosynthesis sentences, in any order. There are several options:

■ After neutralizing the beliefs, you discover that it is indeed impossible to change the situation. In that case, you may address the wish or desire to change the situation. The challenge associated with it may be part of your mission. *C'est la vie*. It is what it is, and what you can't change you must cope with: surrender.

■ You resolve some of the beliefs, reconnect to your innate power, and discover aspects you *can* change. Every step you take out of the limiting situation will open new doors.

The application of the Logosynthesis techniques will restore your connection to Essence, and then the cycle of limiting beliefs will be broken.

DEPENDENCY,
SURRENDER

Turn off your mind, relax and float downstream.
It is not dying, it is not dying.
Lay down all thought, surrender to the Void.
It is shining.

— George Harrison, Tomorrow Never Knows

Dependency is a state of mind in which you hand over control to the people or social systems around you. It's one of the origins of *You Make Me Feel*: Every action, every statement, every expression will automatically generate emotions that match the interaction. If people are friendly, you'll feel good. If they criticize you, you'll feel anxious. If they are indifferent, you'll feel rejected, frozen in shame and guilt. What did you do to lose the love of those you need?

You have handed the power of your Essence to the people around you, expecting that in return they will fulfill the needs of your body and mind—feed you, help you, love you. You hope they will help you survive and save you from utter loneliness if you give them power over you. You become a servant or even a slave, never knowing if, and for what you'll be paid.

Dependency was real when you were a child. Children can't survive without others they can depend on. If needs were not met in childhood, people may try to compensate for this later, finding authorities and organizations who offer security in exchange for their life energy. They are frozen in dependent patterns and will give up freedom for company.

They surrender, but not to the hands of a Divine power that holds them. To be able to surrender to the Divine, you need to become aware of your own divine nature, and to reconnect to your Essence.

George Harrison's "Tomorrow Never Knows" beautifully expresses what is so difficult to grasp in Western cultures: surrender, letting go, giving up control, living in the moment with what is, with those around you who are also just as they are.

Yet you may see the meaning within: It is being.

Logosynthesis helps to restore the flow, helps you to surrender to *All That Is*.

BURNED OUT,
BORED, OR BALANCED?

If fun or action are important enough for you to pursue, you'll need increasing amounts to reach the same level of stimulation. At a certain point, you'll reach the limits of your body and mind, and the accumulated stimulation will burn your candle at both ends.

If your desire for fun and action is not fulfilled, you'll be bored and annoyed. Your life will pass in an attitude of impatient waiting for the next opportunity to do what you enjoy.

If your life situation doesn't offer the right resources for what you consider to be important, you'll feel limited and bound, with contempt for the circumstances that keep you tethered.

Boredom is a state that points to a lack of engagement. You're not in contact with Essence, with your mission in this life. You don't have a task you consider meaningful, and you're bored by the people around you. People tend to avoid responsibility for such a state of mind: They expect others to create a meaningful or at least entertaining experience *for* them. This attitude often breeds self-righteousness and cynicism.

If boredom and meaninglessness continue for a period of time, it can turn into depression. Typically, healthy emotions are absent in a state of depression: no joy, anger, sadness, shame or fear. If you look more closely, you find these emotions are all there, but they have cancelled the expression of each other out.

You cannot be angry and sad at the same time, because you have to focus outwardly to be angry and inwardly to be sad. Anger is connected to aggression, a readiness to fight, but you cannot fight if you're sad simultaneously: sadness leads to withdrawal. There is a turning out and turning in that happens at the same time and creates a paralysis. The same is true for joy and shame. Depression is the state that develops if you feel many emotions simultaneously, and that results in feeling nothing anymore.

Moments of being bored or bound offer opportunities to explore patterns of second order dissociation:

- *What are you doing in order to avoid the deep emptiness and loneliness that results from a disconnection from Essence?*

- *What keeps you running?*

- *What's the worst that could happen if you stopped?*

Once you manage to stay in tune with Essence, life is new every day. What you need in order to discover and live your purpose will be made available, in surprising ways.

Logosynthesis can support you in resolving these issues.

Are you experiencing fatigue and exhaustion?

If yes, do you recognize yourself in the following pattern?

1. You're working hard for a valid purpose, and you want to do it right.

2. You don't rest during natural break times: you work evenings, weekends and on vacation.

3. In childhood you were conditioned to try hard, but when you did, the results were seldom good enough for praise. Instead, the bar was raised, and you were pushed to achieve even greater results.

It may be obvious that you get tired when your body doesn't get proper rest, but the common advice to get that rest does nothing to alter this pattern. When your body pulls the metaphorical emergency brake by becoming ill or creating an accident, you might recognize this as a signal to rest. The disease or the accident is forcing you to rest, but after being discharged from the hospital, the pattern restarts. Why?

The reason is that your seemingly noble purpose isn't motivated from the source of your life energy, from your Essence. It's a permanent striving to be seen as good in the eyes of your parents. The wish to be seen, accepted, respected and loved may grow more intense when in the past you have created frozen images of people who don't love you. You believe that they only saw you if you achieved something and even then, it wasn't good enough. Even when you engaged in a noble goal, achieving that goal wasn't enough; there was always a need for recognition. You learned you need others to make you feel good.

As long as a part of you is driven by the hidden need or hope for recognition, you can't stop without being confronted with feelings of abandonment. Therefore, you keep long hours and work beyond your job description because this helps you to avoid the pain. In this pattern, work as well as fatigue become creative solutions to avoid the pain of rejection, neglect and abandonment. Nights, weekends and vacations would be a lonely hell if you weren't too exhausted to notice.

Your doctor's advice to rest won't solve the underlying problem. Medication, drugs or alcohol won't solve it either. These are simply alternative ways to cover up the pain of the past, of not being seen or heard. In this pattern, the risk of substance abuse is always present.

There is an alternative to trying to get more attention from others by demonstrating how exhausted you are, how hard you work. You are better off treating the past trauma that led to the rejecting images' creation, the subsequent loss of safety, and the longing to be loved.

The real solution lies in the identification, localization and resolution of the energy structures that keep judging you and your work: You don't need anyone to make you OK, you are OK from the start. If your personal space is filled with the energy structures of people who tried to link your work and your being good enough, that's the place to start applying the Logosynthesis sentences.

Identify these images, voices and felt presences, find them in your personal space and process them with the sentences, one after the other. There may be hundreds of them, because the messages about what gave you value were repeated again and again, as a child by parents and teachers, as an adult by bosses and colleagues. In this way you can start loving and stop longing.

Once you discover that your value is not determined by what others think of you, your awareness of Essence will increase, and your real purpose will crystallize. Once that purpose is clear it becomes easier to use your resources without exhausting them.

Even God took a rest after six days of creation.
Why shouldn't you?

If you seek guidance, in coaching, counseling or psycho-therapy, it's probably because you are suffering from some-thing. You have conflicts in the workplace, you have lost the love of another, you have financial problems, or your health is in jeopardy. You need help, and so you start on a journey to change your life.

Most people are reluctant to recognize their own role in the issue they're suffering from. They feel as if it's happening to them; they can't help it. They're the ones doing their best, the helpless victims of circumstance, while others make mistakes or have faults. *You Make Me Feel* is an unquestioned part of their life. They fear everything will get worse and they won't be able to do anything to stop it. Does this sound familiar to you?

When you're entering a healing process—in the sense of becoming whole again—you tend to focus on problems you experience in the present, and you want a professional to solve the problem, to remove it from your life.

Your coach, psychotherapist, counselor, let's call them the *guide* here, will listen to you with patience and acceptance, without judging or trying to change anything. It takes a while for you to feel welcome, to realize this is a safe place, that the guide is there for you and only for you—in this session at least.

This is where healing starts. The fog created by your defens-es is clearing, and a deeper level of the issues comes to the surface. The presence of the supportive guide leads to the realization that those around you are not so supportive. One step further along the way you become aware that even your mother or father were not there for you in this way. On the contrary: Your parents ignored your needs—even ridiculing or rejecting you for having them.

The fact that your guide is present, while others were not, can lead to relief at first: "Finally someone sees me, listens to me." A possible next step is anger. That follows from the thought that if the guide can be here for you now, the others could have been there, should have been there, or could and should be there for you now. The world is not as you want it to be, and you slowly start to realize it never was.

You share that anger with your guide, who quietly accepts it as a first step in the process. Anger is a legitimate and understandable reaction to the fact that your needs were not met, a logical consequence of the belief *You Make Me Feel*. Your guide will react with patience: They know that this anger covers up a still deeper layer that you're not yet able to face. For the moment it feels good to be angry: Your energy level goes up and you're not a victim anymore.

A next step is the realization that life itself has offered neither ideal parents nor an ideal environment. The empty space held by the guide allows a plethora of memories to surface; memories in which you weren't seen, heard, taken care of, loved, in which you were ignored, rejected or even abused. That hurts. The guide reacts to your pain with compassion, but without trying to shoulder your load.

If the professional you're seeing is trained in Logosynthesis, these are the first occasions in which they will introduce the methods. You will learn to identify, localize and neutralize the disturbing memories. Guides trained in other modalities will use the techniques they learned in their training.

The Logosynthesis sentences work like magic. Whole series of memories are neutralized and fall like dominoes, one after the other, fast and easy. Once your subconscious mind discovers that these sentences are able to resolve the past, it doesn't need to repress memories anymore. After every cycle of the sentences you feel less troubled, more open, more relaxed. You let go of the eternal chatter of internal dialogues and find a new place of quiet.

At first, that process looks easy, but gradually your development enters a new stage. Until now, your identity was drawn from those dissociative patterns. The anger, indignation, outrage, pain, grief, shame and guilt has all been yours, has been YOU. When you used the words "I" or "me" in this context, it was clear that these emotions said something about you as a person. You owned the emotions and the emotions owned you.

The next stage of your process the neutralization of painful memories reveals the insight that you have based your frame of reference on fantasies—about how the world could be, should be, could have been or should have been. Now these fantasies enter the foreground to be processed, together with the beliefs connected to them. After every round of the Logosynthesis sentences your conclusion will be the same: *That's life. Sh*t happens. C'est la vie.*

This is where the crisis begins. You discover that the world hasn't been designed to meet your needs. It's not the task of other adults to please you or to take care of you. It's not your task as an adult to please others or to make them happy. Once you realize this, the dawn of a new knowing will arise.

As soon as you feel a negative emotion, a new idea will pop up in your mind: "*This is not ME*" or "*I am not this emotion, even though it feels as though I am.*" Your Self is not caught in frozen energy patterns anymore: It's free, connected to what you really are beyond space and time: Essence. You, as the Self manifested by that Essence, will now meet reality as it is, and you start to recognize your unique potential in this reality.

Before, emotions used to be your most important reference point. If you felt angry, you thought someone else had to do something about it. If you felt sad, you needed someone to comfort you. If you felt guilty or ashamed, you tried to figure out what others expected from you. Now you realize that most of your emotions are irrelevant because they don't apply to what's going on in the present, in your adult life.

This is a *crisis*, in the most literal sense. There's no turning back. What started as therapy now turns into spiritual development. Crisis, an ancient Greek word, originally meant "a decisive moment" in which you assess all relevant information and make a new decision. When you realize that the emotions you are feeling do not reflect the real YOU, you have entered a new and unfamiliar world. In this new world you can explore emotions instead of immediately acting upon them:

- *What do my emotions reveal about my beliefs and expectations?*

- *Do these beliefs and expectations match the reality of the world?*

If you're caught in a traffic jam and you notice yourself getting angry, you may discover a belief that the road belongs to you alone. Such a belief will justify road rage. However, in reality you share the road with others who also paid the taxes which created the infrastructure.

If you fear that people won't like you if you ask for something, a belief may surface that your right to exist is given by others. If you let go of that belief, fear will no longer force you to please others in order to get your needs met. Instead, the experience of fear helps you explore the bedrock of your thinking. Once you discover the foundation, you can apply the Logosynthesis sentences to the memories associated with the fear.

Once you've started this process, you won't really know who you are for a while. You'll be switching back and forth between acting out your emotions and reflecting on them, all the while applying the Logosynthesis sentences to the hopes, wishes, expectations, fantasies and values you discover they're based upon.

If you remove the clutter and continue bravely along the Path, there will be that great reward of times of crisis: You can dedicate your life to the mission of your Self in this life.

HATE MEETS LOVE,
COMPASSION, AND GRATITUDE

Hate and love are the most fundamental states of mind, directly representing the roots of the Logosynthesis philosophy. Hate is the ultimate separation from the Essence of your being. In hatred, you're also separated from other people, because you have nothing in common. You're totally caught in frozen forms of yourself and others. You deny every form of togetherness with other human beings, family, groups, or humanity as a whole.

You've lost touch with the fact that we're all cells of the same organism, branches of the same tree, citizens of the same universe. In hate, there is always something to fight against, you believe that you're not seen in your needs, and this is your only interpretation of what's going on in your life. Under the hard surface of hate lie deeply buried despair and loneliness.

In our Logosynthesis frame of reference, Love is the opposite. You're deeply aware that you are a part of something larger: a spark of the Divine. There is no separation between you and another person, group, society or the universe. You know it's irrelevant because we're all one. You recognize that every being has their own destiny, and you're aware of and feel compassion for that, even if you can't lift someone's burden or if you need to set limits in their best interest. There's a state of *flow*, a free exchange of energy between your Essence and the world you've chosen to live in. There is room for times of calm, ease, peace and quiet, as well as for times of change and challenge.

Love is closely connected to gratitude, the deep realization that something has been given to you for simply being what you really are. Being in love opens a window to the love and gratitude described here. When you're in love with another, you get a taste of how life could really be. Being in love also brings the risk of believing *You Make Me Feel*: believing the other person is the cause of your bliss.

There is a hope, a wish, a desire or an illusion that from now on this person will fulfill the needs of your body and mind. If this is the case, any failure of the other to do so will close more and more of the window to Essence, and eventually love turns to disappointment, irritation, anger, rage and in the end, hate.

Being in love also holds the possibility of opening the door to a deeper understanding of love in the context of Essence, the Divine, Universal Love. Then you can truly meet each other.

For your work in Logosynthesis, the states described here are irrelevant: If someone really hates, you won't be able to access the underlying loneliness and disconnection from Essence. If someone really loves, your job is done. You can even look at what you can learn from them for your Self in this realm of existence.

INDIFFERENCE

Indifference is interesting. At first glance, it seems that nothing is happening. Another person is experiencing intense emotions—whether negative or positive—and you appear uninterested or unaffected. How is that possible if we are all connected?

It looks as if indifference is the opposite state of *You Make Me Feel*. Whatever happens, you don't seem to feel it at all.

From a Logosynthesis viewpoint, indifference actually stems from dissociation. You're not present in the here-and-now, and so you create an impenetrable barrier between yourself and the other person. If we look at it more closely, indifference points to an interruption of the flow of life energy in three possible fields. We define those fields as the *Path of Courage*, the *Path of Trust* and the *Path of the Will*, and in our Practitioner curriculum a seminar is dedicated to each of them.

On the *Path of Courage*, indifference can mean a lack of connection with the suffering of your fellow humans. It leads to the question:

> *What has been so painful in your own life that it caused you to repress your awareness of suffering, not only in your own life, but also in the lives of others?*

On the *Path of Trust*, indifference denies the possibility of experiencing love, tenderness and closeness with other people.

This begs the question:

Which loss of love and affection hurt you so deeply that you're not able to connect and to trust, refusing to share life's ups and downs with other people?

On the *Path of the Will*, indifference means disconnection from life's purpose, the meaning of your existence in this world. We can ask:

What was so discouraging in your life, which perceived failure so traumatic, that you lost awareness of your Divine direction and capacity to follow that path?

SADNESS,
GRIEF

Sadness and grief are deep, elementary emotions which show up if you lose someone or something important. There are two types of natural reactions to this loss:

■ One is to share your experience with the people around you. They will help you to find words to describe what has happened to you and to adapt to the new situation: a world in which the beloved person or object isn't there anymore.

■ In this process, it's also natural to withdraw from the world, in order to process the loss. The loss is at the center of your awareness, and you take the time to let it sink in. You're going through the well-known stages of denial, depression and anger to find a new balance from which to reconnect with the world again.

Sadness and grief result from a tension between the reality of a loss and the wish for an alternate reality, in which the lost person or object is still present. If you're stuck in this process, you can apply the sentences of Logosynthesis to this wish that cannot be fulfilled. In this process you also retrieve your energy bound in representations of the person, the animal, the health or the wealth you have lost.

At first it may seem strange to retrieve your energy from something so positive and important to you, until you realize that you're not taking your energy from the person or object itself, but from the frozen energy construct you created of them. Paradoxically, these emotions tend to soften when you retrieve your energy bound in the desired presence of the person or object.

This application of Logosynthesis allows you to embody fully this current reality, with all its potential for new experiences, new people, and new activities. It allows you to turn from the pain in the past and instead look to the future.

With the help of Logosynthesis you can achieve this. If you suffer from grief, you may need support from a trained professional who offers a safe space for this transition.

If you're a professional, you must realize that a client needs all your love when they start processing grief, and your timing of the intervention must be extremely sensitive, guided by love.

A grieving person seems to be mourning a recent loss—of a partner, a parent, a job, a home or a pet.

In longer conversations with people in grief, it often becomes clear that grief has actually been present in the person's field for a longer time, and the present pain is repeating a much earlier loss—a parent, a grandparent, a sibling, a pet, or even a doll. They can also mourn the loss of a happy family before the parents' divorce, the innocence of childhood, or the bliss of a life before the trauma of an accident, illness, or separation.

The loss embodies the ending of a state of being in contact with another, of being truly seen. Someone enjoyed the real you: You knew it, you felt it, you showed it, and then it was over. Life was never the same after that separation, and you don't expect it to be the same ever again.

If you look closer, the grief is not so much the loss of a person or an object. The loss represents a detachment from Essence, from the flow of life energy itself. That experience of the flow was associated with the presence of someone beloved. It was as if the energy of Essence flowed through the other person to you, as if it was that person who made you happy. You want to be with them again, to return to that state of grace.

What you don't realize is, the love you felt as a child, as a lover, as a brother or sister, was not only what came through the other to you. It was also a mirror of the love that came *from* you, a love now hidden from your awareness. Love is the awareness of Essence in its purest form, the awareness of the beauty of connection.

Grief work in Logosynthesis is about the reconnection to the awareness of what people really are. This process starts with resolving the frozen memories of the trauma that interrupted their felt connection to your Essence, Source, your Higher Self. The police at the door to bring the news of a fatal accident, the frozen images of the child's dying mother, the sound of the shots that killed a husband.

A next step is the addressing the frozen memories of the beloved one. These will stand in the way of being in the present, and everyone and everything now will look bleak and meaningless through the filter of a happier history.

This way of thinking about grief is unusual, and you must be aware that the long-standing relationship with a dearly beloved can prevent one from processing the loss when working with a counselor or psychotherapist. You need to feel very safe with them to be able to retrieve your energy from the frozen memories of those who once opened a window to that state of grace.

The beloved one was not the source; they were the conduit. They showed you that Essence exists, that you *are* love. Letting go of the frozen images of that time will cause love to flow through you in the here-and-now. As you will see in the next chapter, grief will turn to gratitude.

For years I've woken up in the early hours in a panic, feeling paralyzed. I've repeatedly addressed it with Logosynthesis, discovering and resolving various introjects. Gradually this state, and the level of distress, started to shift.

In the beginning, that level was high, close to panic attacks. Later the state changed; it felt more like depression than anxiety. Because depression is nothing but a container for opposing emotions that cancel each other out, I explored these with their triggers and neutralized them in turn: anger, shame, guilt and more. I discovered many Logosynthesis concepts and techniques during those early morning meetings with my destiny.

Over time, I learned to recognize this state as a learning opportunity. I knew there was something new to discover when I awoke in the night. When the distress level finally reached a level of a 2 or a 3, a new emotion appeared: sadness.

What could I be sad about? Everything in my life seemed perfectly ok—in love, work, health and wealth. I didn't know where to look or listen. Suddenly I heard an inner voice saying: "Something is repressing your creativity." I'm familiar with such messages: They're providing guidance, and I take them very seriously.

I didn't have a clue as to what made me sad and repressed my creativity; I had resolved so many aspects of my past and of my environment that there was barely anything left to cause such distress.

I decided to understand and to treat it as a field, and started to test aspects of that field, excluding what it was not. On my right side, there was a kind of cloud a meter in diameter. It was not a field from my own past, nor had it come from a past life, or even a parallel universe. All those had been addressed previously. The sadness was all that remained after countless early morning sessions.

I knew that family trauma can lead to deeply buried emotions. These are expressed as vague physical and emotional symptoms and limiting beliefs, suppressing one's potential and power. I remembered a recent seminar on Logosynthesis and the body. Roger, an old colleague and friend, was suffering from a watery eye, as if he was crying. At 78, that's not unusual, but he suspected there was more to it.

I decided to use a *mapping* technique: I invited Roger to find a place in the room for his right eye, then to become the eye and go back on a time line to find out when it had started crying.

As his eye, Roger became aware that its tears had started long ago when his family fled Russia in the turmoil following the 1917 revolution. The refugees suffered from a lifelong grief for the loss of their home country.

I asked Roger to go back to the spot where he had first located the eye, and to stand on that spot. Then I said the Logosynthesis sentences on behalf of his eye. The eye felt better immediately, especially after the second sentence in which the energy of the refugees was removed from its system. On the next day of the seminar, Roger's tears were gone.

Based on my experiences in this work, I tested if the field of sadness had been created in my father's family. It hadn't. It had developed in my mother's family, when my grandfather had suddenly died in an accident with a steam carousel—*Galloping Horses*—on the way to the local fair. He had fallen off the wagon and under the wheels and died the next day. His accident and death were published in the local newspaper as a single column, four-line article.

The family was struck with grief and fell into poverty on that fatal day in 1928. My grandmother was left with six children under the age of 9, my mother being the oldest daughter. She took care of the baby while my grandmother went to work, and left school as soon as possible to support the family.

The family grief was complicated by shame. Poverty made any education past primary school impossible. Even though my mother was extremely bright she had to go to work in the local bakery until she married my father. My grandmother never overcame the shock and died early, age 66, of a neglected pneumonia.

When I started exploring all of this, yellowed photographs surfaced in my mind and I was overwhelmed by grief. I said the Logosynthesis sentences on behalf of the grieving family in this frozen field. My body shook with the second sentence: A wave of sadness and grief was drawn out of it and sucked into the cloud on my right. After the third sentence, I slept deeply and woke up again at 9:30 am.

Continuing the work, I explored what was left in the frozen field of the family and discovered the presence of my grandfather himself. He was still frozen at the moment of death with the question: "What will happen to my wife and children?" After I had said the sentences on behalf of my grandfather, the distress level went from a ten to a zero and he finally found his peace.

I tested for sources of distress in other members of the family, but the last round seemed to have released it all.

Ever since that early morning session, suppressed creativity hasn't been an issue. I'm moved and at the same time quiet, deeply grateful for the incredible gift of Logosynthesis.

LONGING, NOSTALGIA

I live my life in widening circles
that reach out across the world.
I may not complete this last one
but I give myself to it.

— Rainer Maria Rilke, Book of Hours I, 2

Nostalgia is a tricky state of mind. There's no way in the world to satisfy this craving, because you're longing for a state, a condition, a love, or a situation which no longer exists. You can feel nostalgic at the ending of the initial stage of romantic love, when routines and obligations fill the days of the once passionate couple. You see it after graduation, leaving the "student life" and entering the workforce.

You also see it after leaving a country in search of a better life, especially if the new environment brings more challenges than imagined. The climate, the social life or the home in the old place seemed to offer so much more than this new world. In every city in the world, immigrants from other countries flock together and celebrate the country they left, even generations later.

Age is another area susceptible to nostalgia. Many older people are caught in memories of the beauty of youth—its vigor, its potential, its creativity, its flexibility. They can't make peace with the fact that those times have ended, and they forget the painful side of being young. They don't remember the distress, the loneliness, the despair that is also part of youth.

The most tragic aspect of nostalgia is the absence of any real contact with the present. When you're caught in nostalgia, you refuse to accept the current conditions of your life and their relevance for your mission. You tend to compare the new people, job, or environment with that of your previous life. Your new friends and colleagues will never be able to compete with this romanticized past, and you will tend to withhold your love from them.

Life offers different types of challenges:

1. Your mission:
From Essence you have chosen to fulfill a mission in this life. That mission continues for as long as you live, confronting you with ever new aspects you hadn't yet realized were there. In Rainer Maria Rilke's words, you live your life in ever widening circles. Eventually, you will overcome the current difficulty, but not without wishing things were different, and perhaps also with fear that things may get worse.

2. Trauma:
From the first moment of life, human beings must cope with pain, abandonment, danger, wounds and injuries. These hurt and will take time to heal—if healing is possible. Trauma disrupts the structure of your life and changes your hopes and expectations. It creates a set of painful memories we tend to return to, using them as a reference for how we expect the future to unfold.

3. Frozen wishes:
These build the roots of nostalgia. They relate to the wish that the good things in our life will stay forever. They won't.

If your energy freezes in those wishes, you develop nostalgia: Things, places, love, work, health or wealth of the past are remembered as better, and you see your current situation through the clouded mirror of these golden years. You know those times are over, but you wish they weren't.

Nostalgia must be overcome. There is no alternative. You must draw the simple conclusion that the happy days are gone and there is no turning back. This is not something you can decide rationally, because rational arguments won't change the mind of a nostalgic person.

Why not? It's because the origin of nostalgia lies deep beneath your logical, rational mind, in the depths of your limbic system in the brain, the realm of *fight, flight and freeze*. The world you're nostalgic for lives in these depths as an irrational desire. Letting go of that frozen construct can initiate a process of change, a step out of a frozen past to a present with potential.

Our work with Logosynthesis goes beyond the rational. It starts from the basic assumption that we are Essence, beings beyond space and time, manifesting a life in this world of form—a life with a mission. We are created from an eternal flow of life energy, and this life energy can flow freely or can be frozen in patterns.

In the Logosynthesis paradigm it's better to get or keep your energy flowing—in the service of your mission in this life. If you are aware of your mission, your energy will flow towards its fulfillment. If your energy is frozen, the path is blocked. You must remove those blocks.

However, you may feel ambivalent when it comes to nostalgia. Why would you want to alter your emotions and thoughts about something that felt so good? The answer is simple: It doesn't serve your mission. There is no movement, no process, no development. Every moment, every day spent lost in nostalgia is a repetition of the same pattern.

What makes it so difficult to overcome nostalgia? Again, the answer is simple: the pleasure principle. We tend to avoid the pain, the grief and the despair that accompanies the process of letting go. Nostalgia protects against pain, but to go on with your life, that pain must be processed, not avoided. We must clear out our energy field of the frozen thought forms of the past, in order to create space for a vibrant life in the current moment and to get back on track, in the service of our mission.

To process nostalgia with the help of Logosynthesis you don't need to access and neutralize the sweet memories directly. That's painful and tends to generate a lot of resistance. Instead, you access and process other aspects of the situation. The foremost ones usually are:

■ The reason why you decided to leave the previous relationship, job or environment. How boring, or how difficult was the relationship on a day-to-day basis? How stressful was the job, how annoying the boss? How expensive was the house, how small the apartment, how unsatisfying was life in the village or the city? If you ignore the reasons why you left, nostalgia is just around the corner.

■ Another set of reasons is grounded in the nature of life itself, in an inability or even a refusal to accept the base truth that everything arises and passes away: Children are born, they grow up and leave home, friends and family members die, and everyone grows old. People like to claim an exception to these laws of nature, but such an exception is rarely granted. The rich and beautiful seem to be exempted from those laws, but upon a closer look there are no exceptions.
If reality enters your life, you may be confronted with a limiting belief created by experiences of the past, and life is teaching you something new. The belief may have been that love would last forever, but your partner has met someone else. The belief can be that you will keep the job you love, but economic circumstances have caused it to disappear. The belief may be that you will remain healthy all your life, but an illness has turned everything upside down.

■ The deepest cause of nostalgia is the hidden awareness of your true nature. You are Essence, an immortal Soul, a Higher Self, a child of God. As Pierre Teilhard de Chardin, the French philosopher, put it: "*We are not human beings having a spiritual experience. We are spiritual beings having a human experience.*" You enter this world to learn, to explore, to teach, to develop, to practice, to lead, to serve. For this mission you can access the potential, the talents and the instruments to fulfill it, with the exact body and the right mind for this. Entering this world comes with limitations. You leave a world in which you're in contact with your Divine nature, a world in which you're aware, knowing, omnipotent, omniscient, invulnerable.

These aspects each ask for a different Logosynthesis approach to overcome nostalgia. Again, there are many aspects involved:

■ You may have left a partner because you couldn't stand the daily irritations, the annoying discussions, the contemptuous looks or the daily fights anymore. You may forget this once you are confronted with the loneliness and abandonment of life on your own. You may then remember a relationship in which you were happy, but your energy is bound in repressed aspects of what caused you to leave.

■ You must expand your awareness in order to see the whole picture. You must recognize the part that prompted you to leave the existing relationship, job or situation. To overcome nostalgia you may need help, because it's challenging to un-cover distressing memories on your own. You have to identify the painful part of the decision, focus on a key aspect and neutralize that aspect with the Logosynthesis sentences. You may need quite a few cycles for the many aspects of your de-cision, and it may be helpful if someone guides you through this process.

■ If you're confronted with a situation that wasn't in the script you had written for your life, you can address the beliefs on which that script is based. Many people think that a partner shouldn't leave once they've taken marriage vows. That's a strong belief, because it's heavily reinforced in cultures and religions. *What therefore God hath joined together, let not man put asunder* (Mk 10:5). You can apply the Logosynthesis sentences to that belief and to the society that installed or reinforced that belief.

In a sense, every form of nostalgia is a metaphor or representation for the dilemma on which life itself is based. Deep within ourselves we know that we are divine beings: omnipotent, omniscient, and invulnerable to any earthly discomfort, and it hurts to become aware of the limits of our bodies and minds. Spiritual development brings us closer to the resolution of this deepest cause of nostalgia. Once we manage that, it will probably also offer relief for all other manifestations of this phenomenon.

I COULD HAVE DONE BETTER:
REGRET

The past is just a story we tell ourselves.
— Spike Jonze, Her

You've made a mistake. You made the wrong choice and you know it, and it can't be changed now. Regret is the awareness that you could have done something different than what you decided to do. Your chosen path had unexpected negative consequences, and you discover that the alternative would have been better in the long run.

From a Logosynthesis viewpoint, the experience of regret hinges on a false belief: In hindsight, you believe you had an alternative at the time of your decision. There was none. The reasons for your choice were valid. They dominated at the time you made your decision. Only afterwards did the negative consequences arise.

Maybe you didn't even think. Your actions may have been the continuation of a pattern that had been successful in the past, and so there was no reason to review that pattern which governed your choice. There was no reason for a deeper reflection about the decision to be made.

If you are sadder and wiser now, life has taught you a lesson, in the present and for the future. The mistake has created an additional option available to your conscious mind, and you will recognize that option in the future when faced with a similar decision.

The best way to resolve regret is to find the false belief about an alternative reality that doesn't exist. That belief is something like: *"There was a better alternative at the time I made that decision."* If that were true, then you would have chosen it. Once you've identified this nonexistent reality you can say the three sentences and release yourself from it.

Deborah, a 56-year-old colleague, shared this moving account of regret and how she processed it with the help of a long series of Logosynthesis sentences:

> *At the age of 18 I became pregnant and felt I could not keep the child. Without really getting in touch with my emotions I decided to have an abortion and went through with it immediately. Afterwards, I was relieved to have escaped the fate of being a teenaged mother and went on with my life.*
>
> *5 years went by, I married the father of the unborn baby, and we wanted to have children now. When I could not get pregnant, I was awash in a sea of guilt. We continued to try, without success, but still wanted to start a family. We welcomed a 4-year-old foster son into our family who is still living with me now.*
>
> *When I started working with Logosynthesis on this issue, I immediately felt a sense of guilt and sadness. My level of distress was at 7-8. I addressed the belief: "I am guilty." After the second sentence compassion for the younger me arose for having had little choice at that age. After the third sentence came guilt concerning my foster child. The distress level was at a 7.*

In the next cycle, I applied the sentences on this guilt. In the third sentence I added the words "…as a caring mother." A sense of courage appeared and the distress level lowered to a 4.

The remaining regret of the abortion and distress was still at a level 8. In the third cycle, compassion came up for myself in the situation at the time. My level of distress went down to a 3.

There was guilt left associated with my foster son. The thought came to me: "I have to make it up to him." I ran the fourth cycle with this belief: "I have to make it up to him." To the 3rd sentence I added the words "…as a mother and companion." Then came a longing to have given birth to my son, along with much pain and grief.

The fifth cycle focused on the fantasy of having been constrained by my circumstances at the time. I addressed the belief I would have been estranged from my mother. In the second sentence I sent the non-me energy back to the field of my mother, my great grandmother and my ancestors, and in the third sentence I added: "as a lovable woman." The level of distress was now at a 4.

The last cycle focused on the wish to be less dependent on the reactions of others. After this, the level of distress at a 0. Since then a heavy burden is gone, and my ability to dream and to freely ask for what I want has improved.

RESENTMENT,
BITTERNESS

Resentment is a typical state of mind in *You Make Me Feel*. It is connected to expectations, memories or fantasies. Other people should have seen you, they should have recognized and respected or fulfilled your needs or desires. Fact is, they didn't. There's no way around that fact.

You have invested energy into the relationship the way people invest on the stock market, with the hope of a return on investment. But with this person, in this life, there is none. Whose fault is this? For someone who feels resentful, the fault lies with others. You're OK, but something is wrong with them. You created a rule that that others should be aware of and fulfill your expectations.

Bitterness is the mental state that develops out of an extended period of resentment. A bitter person has stopped expecting a return, and so has decided to stop giving. It's a lonely position, but this loneliness cannot be lifted because all emotional doors through which to connect with others have been closed. You are not OK, nor is the other person.

Resentment and bitterness can only be given up after noticing you were under the illusion of a right or a rule. One recipe is to accept what Frederick Perls, the founder of Gestalt therapy, wrote in his *Gestalt Prayer* (1969):

> *I do my thing and you do your thing.*
> *I am not in this world to live up to your expectations,*
> *And you are not in this world to live up to mine.*

You are you, and I am I, and if by chance we find each
other, it's beautiful.
If not, it can't be helped.

When I first read Fritz Perls' statement, I felt irritated, but it also had a certain charm for me. I had always learned that I should be there for other people, and that was connected to a hope that then other people would be there for me in response. At the time, I strongly believed in *You Make Me Feel*.

Perls' *Gestalt Prayer* was provocative at the time it was written, and from a perspective of love and respect it is unnecessarily crude. It declares a separation between people without offering ways to connect or reconnect. It's the indifferent opposite of *You Make Me Feel*.

Logosynthesis can help you overcome rigid boundaries by identifying and neutralizing the underlying beliefs about what the people around you should deliver. Then you can open your eyes and chose to make contact.

HOW ANGER
LEADS TO SHAME

We have discussed anger as a *second order dissociation* mechanism, a creative solution to not feel trauma, abandonment, fear, rejection or humiliation. People tend to adopt this solution from their parents. Many people express frustration towards their children when they are overwhelmed by their parental responsibility. Small kids can't defend themselves against this anger, and when they grow stronger, they tend to repeat what they themselves have experienced. You feel less frustrated when you can point your finger towards another person: *You Make Me Feel.*

However, this solution comes with its own disadvantages: Once anger is expressed inappropriately it creates more of the same problems it was intended to overcome. People don't like anger. They tend to avoid angry people. They become passive, they pick up the gauntlet thrown at them, or they just turn their back to you. An angry person is therefore a lonely person. Then the angry ones, often men, are thrown back to the original cause of that anger: abandonment, rejection and shame. Not an easy thing to admit.

In a counseling or psychotherapeutic process, now is the time to look at the receiving end of anger: shame. Children subjected to adult anger are dependent. They don't have the opportunity to get a second opinion about their OK-ness. There is no way they can leave an unfriendly environment because their survival depends on the mercy of an angry adult. The child is then frozen in shame; a physical, emotional and cognitive state of the deepest despair and disarray.

Shame is the sudden realization that you have hurt someone, you haven't met an expectation, or you unknowingly transgressed a rule. The person who becomes angry at you for those reasons is someone you rely on for survival. The realization that you've disappointed this special person leads to feelings of deep abandonment.

This process leads to powerful energetic representations of those who caused the original trauma. If your father used to scream at you, his image and voice will stay around as frozen patterns in your personal space. This energy pattern is activated whenever someone is unfriendly, even in your adult life.

As a result, you tend to stop thinking about the hidden expectation forever. It is secretly installed, and even worse: Instead of being re-examined, the expectation is passed on to the next generation without any reflection as to its legitimacy.

Even for an adult, shame is an extremely powerful and unpleasant state of mind. You feel abandoned, excluded. You don't belong, something is utterly wrong with you. You are wrong, false, bad, and at fault.

Logosynthesis enables you to identify, activate and neutralize the frozen representations of the *You Make Me Feel* moments that caused this pattern:

- A parent or a teacher was lonely, powerless and overwhelmed by their responsibilities.

- Anger directed outwards was the only way they could cope with this state of mind.

- The victim of the anger was caught in shame, because they couldn't meet the expectations of the angry authority.

- A representation of the angry person was created in the personal field of the child, entangled with a reaction pattern of shame and powerlessness.

- When the child grew up, expressing anger as a coping pattern was borrowed from the previous generation.

In Logosynthesis we work towards identifying the pain of the wounded child and the environment in which the trauma occurred. Neutralizing the introjects will also resolve the states of mind that have in turn caused the person's current difficulties.

If you're caught in shame, explore the early memories of incidents in which you felt that shame. Find answers to the following questions:

- *When did this happen?*

- *Who was present?*

- *If I think about them now, where do I perceive them in space? In front of me? Behind me? To the left? To the right? Above me? Below me? How far away?*

- *What did I see, hear and sense from that other person?*

- *How did I react then?*

After answering these questions, find the image or the voice of the other person in space, say the three Logosynthesis sentences for that perception, and let the words do the work.

Fear is a healthy emotion as long as a real threat exists. Evolution has designed and developed fear as a response pattern to help you survive in a world full of dangers.

Fear can trigger three types of deeply ingrained reactions: *fight, flight and freeze.* Fight and flight will help you overcome the dangers of the outside world by running away or confronting the danger, freezing is the reaction that helps you to deal with the unavoidable: Your body becomes numbed by stress hormones and you won't feel the fatal blow. All these mechanisms are completely automatic. They're programmed at the deepest level of the brain and not accessible to change by rational thinking.

Fear can become unhealthy when you're activating the memory of a danger that has long past or creating a fantasy of a future threat that hasn't appeared yet—and may never appear. In my experience, there is a close connection between traumatic experiences of the past and the fear of something painful happening in the future.

If you are caught in fear, you're living in a cage. You're frozen in the perceived threat, unable to leave the danger zone. The threat depletes your resources and causes you to feel helpless and exhausted, until you find a safe place with a partner, a friend, a coach, a counselor or a psychotherapist. Then you'll be able to look through the fog that has surrounded you for such a long time.

As soon as you enter a process of personal change in order to overcome the fear, you'll discover those threats are nothing but frozen energy patterns. You'll feel relief, become stronger, and your energy level will rise. You will start to fill your personal space and expand its outer boundaries. You will enjoy your newly discovered power.

Once your own personal space begins to grow, it will necessarily interfere or collide with the personal space of others, and long buried issues will surface in your awareness. New conflicts between you and others will make you realize that the world is not as you want it to be. You have held back needs so firmly you were largely unaware of them. Now you are aware, not only of unfulfilled needs and desires in the present, but also of all those in the past.

This new development activates *You Make Me Feel* patterns. The other person doesn't like your new attitude and shows it. That may be annoying, because you are experiencing true well-being for the first time. You're finally aware that you're entitled to have needs and to have your wishes fulfilled. You decide that times have changed, you're going to stand up and fight for what's important to you. At this point you meet your next challenge.

You're leaving the cage of life-long fear. In your childhood, you learned to adapt to the needs, desires and wishes of others, but missed learning the checks and balances required to assess what others need in relation to what you need. You haven't learned the intricate game of negotiation between two or more people who interact as adults, with equal rights and equal resources.

In negotiations there is give and take, but since you've been giving all this time you tend to think that now is your time for taking: *Now It's My Turn*. That's an illusion, and those around you won't appreciate it. They will resist fulfilling your needs because they sense your issue isn't about them.

There's no cooperation possible right now. You're obsessed with getting what you want, and you're unaware that some needs can no longer be fulfilled, ever. Those around you may even have liked the prior state in which you were their faithful servant and refuse to relinquish their master role. This can be confusing for you.

The others' reactions can reactivate that old familiar fear; it feels as if nothing has changed. If you explore this process thoroughly, you will recognize that those around you can fulfil some needs, but not all. What starts with anger, ends with grief:

■ You become aware of unfulfilled needs of your past, and you must recognize that no one in your present life will ever be able to meet them.

■ You accept that you didn't have, don't have and will never have ideal parents, siblings, teachers and bosses, and that your spouse, your friends or your colleagues are not in this world to compensate for the deficits of your past.

■ You're giving up fantasies about the world and its people: how they should be, could be, should have been or could have been.

Once you've reached that level of awareness, grief will surface; the grief that you didn't get what you needed—Nobody was there for you in those painful times.

If you're not familiar with Logosynthesis techniques yet, I recommend that you study the summary on page 129-133 of this book first. Others can use the following Logosynthesis sentences to resolve the power of the wishes:

1. *I retrieve all my energy, bound in the wish that this need would be fulfilled, and take it to the right place in my Self.*

2. *I remove all non-me energy related to the fulfillment of this wish, from all of my cells, all of my body and my personal space, and send it to wherever it may belong.*

3. *I retrieve all my energy, bound all my reactions to the fact that this wish hasn't been fulfilled, and take it to the right place in my Self.*

If you're in for a tougher challenge, you can add a variation of the third sentence:

I retrieve all my energy, bound all my reactions to the fact that this wish hasn't been fulfilled, is not fulfilled and will probably never be fulfilled, and take it to the right place in my Self.

Even though trauma of loneliness and rejection is not accessible to your rational mind, it can remain stuck in your energy system for many years. An experienced professional in Logosynthesis can help you release the frozen energy bound up in these early experiences. Then you'll reconnect to the source of what you really are: Essence.

ANGER
AND DISSOCIATION

Angie was in training to become a Practitioner in Logo-synthesis. One part of this process is to become aware of and resolve one's own frozen emotions. This was when Angie wrote me:

> *As I zero in on all those automatic reactions using Logosynthesis I am experiencing a lot of anger, especially as those frozen states dissolve, leaving examples of where my boundaries where invaded. The childlike states seem by their nature passive.*

My answer:

> *Anger is the emotion you feel when you notice a threat to yourself, to the people you care about, or to your values or possessions. Anger will trigger behavior aimed towards removing the threat. Sometimes that's healthy. It becomes unhealthy if the anger contains the implied expectation that other people should be aware of, respect, and meet your needs.*

So, if you're angry at someone, explore these expectations as the first step:

- *Is the other person aware of how I want to be treated?*

- *Are they interested in learning how I want to be treated?*

- *Is this the appropriate person to understand and meet my needs?*

If the answer is a triple *no*, the emotion experienced as anger is usually a cover for deep feelings of loneliness and abandonment. Then it's time to explore if the person involved triggers early emotions related to unfulfilled needs, especially early in your life.

There are different levels of negative emotions:

1. Emotions directly associated with trauma and abandonment, like shame, guilt, apathy, sadness and fear. These emotions tend to make you think, feel and act from the position of *"I'm not OK, something is wrong with me."* Trauma, rejection and abandonment are experienced viscerally, and you feel excluded from the community. With these emotions, the person is frozen, passive. In Logosynthesis we call this first order dissociation.

2. Emotions to cover up those under (1). Here the roles are often reversed: *"I'm OK, and You're Not."* This is the specter of anger, rage, arrogance and pride. Dominant behavior is expressed, and you associate your feelings with the faults of the other. In Logosynthesis we call this second order dissociation, and the corresponding behavior is active, dominant.

If you look at these patterns more closely, the second order dissociation is clearly a compensation for the first, a creative adaptation to the fact that the emotions of first order dissociation are simply unbearable. Children are smart, and they learn fast. They observe the behavior of their caregivers, see that they don't suffer, and as soon as they have grown strong enough, borrow their parents' behavior patterns as a solution to escape from the distress and pain of abandonment. Thus, beaten boys become abusive fathers.

Anger, arrogance and pride are relatively pleasant emotions compared to those associated with first order dissociation.

The person feels entitled to aggressively defend their perceived boundaries and can even be proud of that aggression. You can observe this behavior often and everywhere at this time in history.

Anger is omnipresent, and the question arises of how we can cope with it from both positions: when we are angry at others and when others are angry at us. For adequate de-escalation we must explore both.

We learn about anger early in life. Children don't always behave, and parents are not always able to patiently teach them the rules of society. In such moments the stress level rises, and when that happens, anger is not far away.

Anger is an evolutionary mechanism designed to defend a territory. In this process animals can be hurt or killed in the service of survival. Humanity has perfected this skill along a spectrum; with weapons and walls on one side and sophisticated judicial systems on the other. This has allowed us to inhabit the earth in large numbers without constant fighting.

However, the biological roots of anger are still present. The *amygdala*, the little almond in the limbic system of the brain is still just as active as it was in humanity's early days. We have an amazing cortex and frontal brain, but we can still become angry in a fraction of a second and bypass the rational thinking we've developed over thousands of years.

This interface between nature and culture is the challenge of every human being. We've created codes to tame our biological inclinations: religions, ethics, laws and moral rules.

Paradoxically we often learn—as well as teach—those codes with the dubious help of impatience, irritation, anger, and even rage.

With the help of anger, people can avoid the feelings of exclusion and abandonment, which are stored in one's personal space as separate energy structures. They create a split: an angry part that feels good and strong in order to avoid experiencing another part that's feeling weak and lonely.

Once such people are grown up, they keep defending themselves against the pain of the underlying trauma. They bring the suppressed anger and rage of their childhood into the open. Here the trouble begins. In suppressing vulnerability in themselves, people also suppress it in those still weak and vulnerable: their children.

Angry people teach their kids that it's not OK to be small or to feel hurt. They are not able to teach their children to trust others and to become aware of their mission, their potential, their skills. In such families, anger loses its evolutionary function to defend and instead becomes an instrument to install the rules of the field in the next generation.

A person will stay locked in this pattern as long as their children, spouses, employees accommodate this anger. However, the anger can really become a problem if the other person is a healthy adult who responds with respectful compassion: *"Why are you so angry?"* Only this attitude can lead to change because it allows the person to experience being seen and respected.

If the emotions and behavior of the destructive pattern are successfully mirrored, the person will become aware of their inappropriate behavior: "*I've beaten my own child.*"

The old feelings of shame and guilt become activated as reactions to the current environment. The person is reenacting the original "*I'm not OK – You're OK*" position, or even the desperate "*I'm not OK – You're not OK*" position. That's the moment real change can take place. In Logosynthesis, the insight that the creative adaptation doesn't work anymore and has become its own problem is called *third order dissociation*. In a nutshell:

- First order dissociation: "*I'm in pain.*"

- Second order dissociation: "*I'm angry because I've been hurt.*"

- Third order dissociation: "*I'm in trouble because I'm angry.*"

I estimate that 90% of all angry outbursts are cases of second order dissociation, and not defensive responses to a real threat. That anger may have been justified in the childhood situation the person has lived through, but it is totally irrelevant when dealing with real people in the present.

Anger is often associated with a recurring grandiose fantasy that those around them should fulfill the needs that their parents did not. They should not. They should not even try.

Once people learn to accept responsibility for their bullying behavior, they can develop new behavior from a position of love and respect which their parents weren't able to offer.

Logosynthesis can neutralize the painful memories which are the roots of rage. Thereafter you will have the freedom to decide if you really want to be aggressive or defensive; this time, based on rational assessment and not on knee-jerk reactions.

You can also search for the magical fantasies behind anger. An example of this is road rage. If you get angry at another driver on the road—he either drives too slow or too fast— this means you're imagining that the road is yours and that the other person is invading your space. The Logosynthesis sentences for this fantasy will resolve the rage and let the insight emerge that the road is there for all to share. Another fantasy connected to road rage is that people should behave rationally, like yourself.

Recently I was caught in a traffic jam. An old man had caused an accident by driving in the wrong direction on the only highway in the valley, and everything was at a standstill for hours. It took me three hours to drive six kilometers. Because I had worked on this fantasy a number of times, I relaxed, went quietly through my emails, and when my phone died, leaned back and listened to the radio.

Another driver got a serious attack of *You Make Me Feel*. He wrote a raging letter to the editor of the local newspaper in which he bitterly complained that the police should have prevented that traffic jam. Yet another driver found a really creative solution. He was enroute with a pallet of water bottles, took them out of his trunk, walked along the line of cars and sold them all.

AVARICE AND GREED VS.
ABUNDANCE AND GENEROSITY

Avarice and greed are lonely solutions. *Avaritia* was one of eight stumbling blocks on the Path to the Divine, as described by Evagrius Ponticus, a monk in the Alexandrian desert during the fifth century AD. Other monks in the desert went to him for support; today he would be a counselor or spiritual teacher.

Avarice was considered a block on the path to reconnection with God, because it is based on the belief that no one will be there when you're old, weak and in need. You don't want to share with those who are in need now because you believe you will need the possessions yourself later. Later in history, avarice became one of the Seven Deadly Sins that kept the gates of Heaven closed forever.

Greed replaces the purpose and meaning of life in the vertical dimension with collecting material goods in the horizontal. Those goods seems to provide security and comfort, but they lack meaning in themselves. No amount of money and possessions will create a life of purpose. As a result, you'll experience an inner emptiness instead of the expected satisfaction and fulfilment. When your possessions disappear, the loneliness and pain of early abandonment will surface.

If you're in contact with Essence, you're aware that life energy is a never-ending flow. There is always enough, even if your possessions don't fulfil our society's criteria of what a human being should have. When in contact with Essence, it's easy to share with those who are near you and in need. Abundance and generosity stem directly from the flow.

To reconnect with Essence, it's important to access the fear of the future. You can explore what's the worst that can happen in that imagined future:

- Identify the client's immediate distressing fantasy.

- Find the client's worst scenario by asking again and again, insisting on an ever more unpleasant answer: *What's the worst that could happen next if this happened?*

- Only stop asking the question if the client imagines death or deep abandonment.

- Then give the Logosynthesis sentences for the scene discovered in the fantasy or in the memory that shows up.

Addressing the distressing fantasy with the Logosynthesis sentences will lift the fear of loss and loneliness, creating a space for the future to unfold, one of abundance and generosity.

OBJECTS OF DESIRE
ENVY

Be yourself. Everyone else is taken.
— Oscar Wilde

We live in the Rhine Valley in Switzerland, where the climate is heavily influenced by the *föhn*, a warm wind that blows over the Alps from the South. The föhn triggers migraines in those who are sensitive, but it's also called "the grape boiler," because it warms the vineyards on the sunny slopes, helping to grow the best Pinot Noir in Switzerland. In my town there is a saying:

> *The oldest inhabitant of the Rhine Valley is the föhn, the second oldest one is envy.*

Envy is not limited to the Rhine valley. It's the younger sibling of jealousy—less intense and destructive, but still annoying. Another person has something you don't: an object, a relationship or a talent. That activates *You Make Me Feel*: disappointed, sad, ashamed or angry. Envy is not a state which is easy to admit or even access, because many parents teach their children early on that envy is bad and they shouldn't be envious. However, such an admonishment won't abolish envy, it will only drive it into hiding or cover it with other, more acceptable emotions like sadness or anger.

Envy is a state in which another person possesses power, love, health, money or other resources you never had, would like to have, that you have lost and wish to regain, or which you believe you need to be happy. You feel bad while someone else feels good or better than you do. In being envious, you ignore two things:

■ You have all the resources you need for your own task in this life. Destiny will take care that these are delivered to you along with this task.

■ The other person may have or has had their own challenges, which are not obvious to you.

In Logosynthesis terms, envy means you're disconnected from Essence and that your energy is bound up in a desired object or state.

You may not always be aware of envy. If you feel consistently sad or angry in the presence of another person, a hidden envy may be one of the reasons for it. Do you believe that the other is better than you, or they live in more pleasant circumstances? Do they have a better job or more education? Is their house bigger, their garden sunnier or their car faster? Are they wiser, smarter or more attractive? Do they have a larger circle of friends or throw parties more often?

Envy confronts you with a deeply felt deficit, a minus, and the first step towards coping with it is to admit you're different from the other person. Once you recognize and admit that differences are a part of life, you can start to explore their nature and find a way to cope with the envy. This process may contain a silver lining: the discovery of your own unique being, and therewith of your own mission.

Envy informs you that something is important for you, that something mirrored by the other person is relevant—for you, your destiny, your purpose. You may not have achieved or even discovered that purpose yet. You're distracted by the destiny of others, and you notice a painful tension between where you are and where you want to be. Those who activate your envy issue don't feel that tension. They already have what they want.

Envy is a sign that energy is bound in a wish, a desire, a hope that you'll have or be the same as another. This wish is the translation of your own destiny into the form the other person has created for theirs. If your neighbor has a Ferrari and you envy him, this implies the belief that his fulfilled wish is your unfulfilled one.

This belief is a distortion of reality. It only means that you're not aware of your destiny yet, because on the level of Essence, no one is the same or needs the same things. At the same time, the perceived importance of your neighbor's Ferrari provides you with useful information about next steps in your personal and spiritual development. It tells you clearly that you have to switch your attention from your neighbor's possessions to your own hidden gifts.

Envy means you're out of touch with your Self, and in turn with your reason to be here on this blue planet. Johann Wolfgang von Goethe points this out beautifully in *Polyhymnia*:

> *For our wishes often hide from ourselves the object we wish for; Gifts come down from above in the shapes appointed by Heaven.*

If you're in touch with Heaven, nothing can make you envious, because you live your mission, your purpose, your way of being. Comparison becomes irrelevant. I've written before that life's most important questions are "*Why are you here?*" and "*What keeps you from living that mission?*"

In Logosynthesis terms, envy binds life energy in representations of other people and their characteristics or possessions, which in turn activates an unfulfilled wish of yours. If you want to discover the gifts hidden for you in that wish, here's the Logosynthesis strategy, elegant as always:

■ Find out what exactly in the other person makes you envious.

■ Create an imaginary video of the other person with the object or characteristic you're longing for.

■ Apply the Logosynthesis sentences on that video.

■ Notice how your focus shifts from the other person to you, to your Self. If other issues show up, repeat the procedure.

JEALOUSY,
THE MANY-HEADED DRAGON

Jealousy is a many-headed dragon. There are many names for its heads: anger, sadness, grief, guilt, shame, disgust, hope and fear. Like *Hydra*, the monster in a Greek myth, two new heads appear for every head you cut off.

In another metaphor for jealousy, you're sucked into a maelstrom of emotions, thoughts, values, memories, fantasies and beliefs, and it feels impossible to reach solid ground. You cannot think straight.

Jealousy is a state of mind beyond rational understanding as well as self-control. It pulls the rug out from under your feet. It feels so unsettling that you need metaphors to grasp this phenomenon, and these metaphors offer insights and ways to cope with it.

However, the metaphors mentioned above reveal a general helplessness when it comes to finding your way out of jealousy. Only brave knights manage to tame dragons or to slay them, and jealous people are not brave. They're angry, mean, sad or shaken.

These metaphors suggest that if you're confronted with jealousy, there is no easy way out, no linear technique or fail-safe method. When you experience jealousy, it's difficult to explore your state of mind beyond pain, vulnerability, anger and rage, especially if you put the cause of the problem squarely onto your partner.

From a Logosynthesis viewpoint, jealousy is a frozen conglomerate of emotions and beliefs:

■ A belief that you need another person in order to feel happy: You're not an autonomous person.

■ A belief that the other person needs to be, to behave, or to perform in certain ways for you to be happy. You also don't perceive the other person as autonomous.

■ A belief that you must be or do something to make the other person give you what you need: The relationship is seen as a contract based on the exchange of services.

■ A belief that another person has certain qualities that you lack: love, power, money, sex, youth, attention, intelligence.

■ A fantasy that in the end you'll be rejected.

All these components of jealousy are forms of disconnection from Essence. You try to use the relationship to compensate for that loss and to cover up the loneliness of your existence. The relationship is your only window to Essence, and your partner threatens to close it by leaving you.

Jealousy is complex. It freezes your personal and spiritual development. That's not all: Your state is further complicated by society, which endorses and reinforces all the above beliefs and fantasies. It established marriage as a cell within larger societal organisms like extended families and neighborhoods.

Logosynthesis reconnects you to reality. You learn to accept shortcomings of yourself and the other. Reconnection with Essence can either lead to reconciliation or to separation.

As a professional working with jealousy issues, you may experience strong countertransference reactions, from deep compassion to intense loathing. These reactions can overwhelm you and make you feel helpless. I recommend you explore them in a moment of solitude or in supervision with an experienced colleague.

How do we deal with jealousy from an energy perspective, from a Logosynthesis viewpoint? The short answer is that we must interpret it as an expression of frozen energy, because you're suffering. If your energy would be in flow, there would be able to stay calm. That explanation may seem theoretical and unhelpful, but it can help you to understand what's going on from an energy point of view. If you assume that energy can be frozen then you also know that energy can be in flow. So, let's follow this line of reasoning.

In Logosynthesis, energy can be frozen in stored or imagined perceptions of your world—memories and fantasies. Energy can also be frozen in beliefs that result from or relate to these archaic or imagined perceptions. The beliefs of a jealous person mirror the typical *You Make Me Feel* attitude: "*You belong to me*", "*You hurt me*", "*I can't live without you.*" Frozen memories, fantasies or beliefs are entangled with frozen reactions: emotions, obsessive thoughts, and unpleasant body symptoms.

Jealousy tends to tip the balance in a relationship, causing intense emotions on both sides. As long as *You Make Me Feel* dominates your belief system, there is only a faint chance that anything will ever change for the better. It is more likely that the situation will escalate.

There is no shortcut around examining your own process, and once you do that, you will discover that jealousy is not a singular emotion. It's an intricate knot of multiple energy patterns: memories, fantasies and beliefs, interacting with each other in a variety of ways—all the while flooding you with emotions. You can resolve one pattern after the other by applying the Logosynthesis sentences to them.

When working with jealousy, your own or your client's, you can expect a variety of emotions, each with its own triggers:

■ **Fear:**
You imagine being lonely, abandoned, excluded, rejected.

■ **Anger:**
You expect that your partner will behave in your preferred way, and they don't.

■ **Grief:**
You finally realize that a happier time in your relationship is over.

■ **Regret:**
You're aware that you have insulted and violated the other and wish you hadn't.

■ **Shame:**
You realize that you're unable to fulfill the needs of your partner.

■ **Guilt:**
You're aware that you have hurt your partner in the past or have not given them your best.

All these emotions with their corresponding thoughts and behavior patterns are human. Identifying and processing their presence requires a deeply compassionate working relationship, rooted in Essence. From that base it's possible to regain access to a reality in which it's possible to love and be loved, even though this may not be possible in one's current relationship. You may seek support in going through this process: You're not alone.

Each of the states mentioned above most likely is rooted in earlier experiences, when you were too young to grasp what was going on and no one was there to teach you what life is all about. You can learn that now.

Meeting the Rebel To be kind is more important than to be right.
Many times, what people need is
not a brilliant mind that speaks
but a special heart that listens.
— F. Scott Fitzgerald

You're a rebel. You're not like the others and you don't want
to be. You don't want to depend on anyone else. You resist.
You think you're autonomous, and you assert that autonomy.
It may look like autonomy, but your view of the world is
shrunken to a polarity. It's you against all others. You're living
in a world full of people that can hurt you and you invest
energy to avoid being hurt by those people.

You were hurt before; there were people who didn't recognize
your Essence, didn't meet your needs, didn't help you to create
a path for your Essence into the world. You learned to defend
yourself against not only those who hurt you, but against all
people. You're living in a constant fear that what happened
will happen again, and you've decided you won't let it. That
resistance keeps you out of real intimate relationships, which
are based on mutual trust.

Rebels have an important function in the world. They don't
take anything for granted and they challenge established
authorities to look and listen. Sometimes that works, but
sometimes it doesn't, and the rebel ends up resentful and
bitter. To be a successful rebel, you must amass power by connecting with others who share your vision, and you must be
able to negotiate with those you don't agree with. Therefore,

you need to be committed to your own mission, but you must understand that others also come from Essence. Only then you can meet them on equal ground. No authority will ever listen to you if you don't respect it in the first place.

You can't respect anyone as long as you believe that the world, and everybody in it, is against you and your intentions. As long as you hold that belief, people will make you feel bad, and your responses to them will be based in conflict, which in turn doesn't invite others to be kind or collaborative. Carl Gustav Jung wrote:

What we resist, persists.

But we can also say:

What we resolve, evolves.

Logosynthesis helps you to resolve. You will finally give up resistance if someone else gently welcomes you in, with all the mistakes you've made, all the pain beneath your tough mask. That implosion will hurt at first, but then you'll discover that it's only your body or your mind that can be hurt—and you're more than a body and mind: You're Essence. And then you'll learn to dance.

PRIDE, SATISFACTION,
SELF-CONFIDENCE

In the Christian catalogue of deadly sins pride is most damaging to your immortal Soul. Pride puts you on an assumed "higher" level and not only separates you from others in this world, but also from the Divine, from Essence. In its Greek version, *hybris*, it's always the predecessor of *nemesis*, the total breakdown.

A proud person is dissociated from Essence and therefore measures their existential meaning or value in terms of possessions, status, achievements or power. They need things of which to be proud. Under the surface of this pride there is a deep loneliness, and the proud person can never be sure when, how and where this abandoned part will take over.

Pride is different from satisfaction, a state of having reached a milestone, enjoying it, and taking a break. Self-confidence is the trust you derive from your free Self.

You're aware of your mission, your contribution to life on earth. This gives meaning to your life. Real self-confidence may vary with the degree of your contact with Essence, but it will never lead to your ruin.

A proud person will not become a client in counseling or psychotherapy as long as they are successful at shielding themselves from hidden loneliness. They are willing to go to great lengths to avoid the pain, but once their shell is torn, they need an enormous amount of safety in order to explore the deepest levels of the dissociation.

Never try to repair the shell. That's time wasted on the Path.

SELF-RIGHTEOUSNESS, CONTEMPT,
CYNICISM, SARCASM, ARROGANCE

These states are all variations of pride. If you're in one of these states, you're coming from the basic position that you're better than everyone else: *You're OK* and others are not. You think you're better and that entitles you to put others down. These states are other manifestations of the first primal sin mentioned above: pride or *superbia*. The person has to continually collect power, status, wealth and admiration in order to compensate for the abandonment they feel inside.

People in these states are focused on their own needs and thereby limited in their capacity for intimate relationships with other people. Their close relationships are characterized by dominance and submission, without offering safety to their submissive partner.

The self-righteous recreate their early childhood relationships as adults, and you can guess what these looked like: Under this self-righteous layer there is a deep loneliness due to an early disconnection from Essence, which cannot be shown or shared, and thus never lifted.

The life experience of the parents didn't allow for contact with Essence. They were living in a world in which you had to fight to survive, in a world without love, and the child adopted their strategy. That strategy can be successful for a long time, because it's associated with powerful methods to acquire power and hold onto it.

Robert Monroe, a pioneer in the investigation of human consciousness and founder of the Monroe Institute in Faber, VA, wrote:

Reclaiming Your Energy from Your Emotions **95**

Without realizing it, leader-bosses show others how to take bites out of their fellow humans without killing. We've made an art and a science of predation, intraspecies variety.

People in these states of mind don't show up in the consulting rooms of counselors and psychotherapists. They will only seek treatment or support from others when the defensive pattern is disrupted, through the loss of wealth, power or youth. Their first goal will then be to restore the pattern, not to explore it. Once loneliness can surface in the safe container of a strong working alliance, they can begin to resolve the frozen patterns that led to this state.

If you're a professional in guided change, you'll see many clients who are challenged to find ways to cope with the behavior described in this chapter. It might help them to see the loneliness and poverty behind the façade of the perpetrator.

COURAGE

The effort needed to see things without distortion
takes something very like courage;
and this courage is essential to the artist,
who has to look at everything
as though he saw it for the first time:
he has to look at life as he did when he was a child and,
if he loses that faculty, he cannot express himself
in an original, that is, a personal way.

— Henri Matisse, 1954

Courage represents the new. It marks the transition from frozen energy, bound in negative emotions, memories, fantasies and beliefs, into a free state. Courage leaves behind what has been, could have been, should have been, could be or should be. It provides the freedom *to be with what is*, to take the risk of following your mission.

Courage is a special phenomenon. It's the most direct expression of what you really are, living your mission, and it's not surprising that the author of the quote above is an artist. You can't be an artist without being courageous. Real artists don't follow the beaten track. They make their own way in uncharted territory.

If people call you courageous, they mean you'll go to great lengths to follow your perceived destiny and be willing to take great risks in the face of small odds. If you succeed, you'll be considered courageous, if you don't, people will call you foolish. So, strangely enough, being seen as courageous depends on your results.

Truly courageous people don't think much about their own courage. They see what they've done as their task, and their contribution doesn't make them a hero. A courageous person considers taking a risk to reach a goal, their goal in this very moment in contact with Essence, in the service of their mission on this planet. If you call yourself courageous, people will shrug their shoulders see you as adolescent, arrogant or narcissistic.

If you lack courage on your life path, you'll have to explore what it is that you really want. Your mission may have been obscured by patterns you developed to avoid feeling the pain frozen in your field from an earlier stage of life. If you're caught in the compulsion to be strong, to be perfect, to work hard or to please others, it makes it difficult to discover what's really yours in this life.

Earlier in your life, these were useful mechanisms that helped you to survive a lack of love, compassion or support, and it's a good thing they did. The next step in your development is to discover that the power of your Essence is what keeps you alive and gives real meaning to your life, far beyond attention from others. Logosynthesis can help you to find your purpose and to pave your path to its fulfillment.

FORGIVENESS

My colleague Harlow wrote me:

"The question is what role does forgiveness play in this? So often forgiveness is peddled as a cure all. It often appears as condonation. I am often intrigued when people who have been victimized are quick to "forgive" without processing or validating their feelings."

Forgiveness is a somewhat cloudy concept, and I'm grateful to Harlow for inviting me to consider it. Ideally, if energy is freely flowing, forgiveness is the expression of love and understanding by a person who has suffered at the hands of someone else. In Harlow's words this is a "cure all." But the world is not ideal, and that is what makes forgiveness so elusive.

To conceptualize this phenomenon, the English language offers a range of expressions: *Sorry, Excuse me, I apologize* and *Forgive me. Sorry* and *Excuse me* are used to cushion the impact of everyday intrusions, while *Forgive me* is reserved for more serious matters. Apologizing falls somewhere in the middle.

If you look closely at our word excuse, you'll recognize its Latin root causa, which means cause. If you ex-cuse yourself, you take yourself as a c(a)use out of the trouble. The opposite of excusing is ac-cusing, in which you put the c(a)use of a discomfort on the other person.

If person A apologizes to person B, that ritual is often so powerful that it's almost impossible for B to refuse the intrusion of A without being considered rude. At first sight, person A seems to have the role of a humble underdog in the situation, but if we look closely, person A could just as well be the top dog, manipulating B into adaptive behavior: "*Excuse me, could I ask you for a cigarette?*"

If an everyday excuse is already difficult to refuse or defend against, it is even more so when serious damage has been done: The husband who has an affair, or the politician caught taking bribes lack credibility when they beg for forgiveness. If you hear a teenager say sorry after being pushed to apologize, you hear what they say, but you don't buy into it.

Why not? Because you know it's fake. The adolescent wants freedom but is still dependent on his parents. A husband really loves his wife and appreciates everything she offers, but another part of him has other desires. The wife has similar, complementing parts. She desperately wants to be loved and to believe him, another part simply doesn't: So she has a reason to be angry: *You Make Me Feel.* These dissociated parts are rarely integrated through routine forgiveness.

It's this dissociative dimension that makes forgiveness so irritating. We're not naïve; we all know that forgiveness isn't a panacea, but it would be so nice if it was. It's a seductive fantasy that if we really forgave, everything would be forgotten. It's not, it's only covered in a cloak of charity, and nothing is healed in the long run.

The matter becomes even more complicated because forgiveness is labeled as good, noble, or even superior in the context of morality and religion. Christianity teaches us to *turn the other cheek* if someone hurts us, and sinners are forgiven once they confess and practice humility and repentance.

The split is clear: One part wants to express their anger at that sinner and another "holier" part *should* act against that inclination. This will only work for a limited time: the frontal brain can't hold out against the limbic system for longer than a few days or weeks.

For these reasons I avoid the word forgiveness in my work. When it comes to restoring the balance in a current relationship, I prefer the concept of *reconnecting*. The following process will create a completely different future from a standard apology given to save your skin.

Reconnecting is a process after something has gone wrong, both parties suffer from the consequences, and both want to limit the damage. Each partner takes responsibility for their own role in this dis-connection. Questions arise:

■ *Which signs did I miss, caught up in my own fears, needs, wishes, desires, expectations, fantasies, memories or beliefs?*

■ *What changes did I go through that I didn't communicate?*

In this exploration frozen energy patterns will emerge from the depths of your unconscious mind. Memories of an earlier abandonment or rejection can surface and be neutralized, unfulfilled childhood needs on both sides must be faced and left behind.

Both partners must admit that they have not managed their experiences in a loving, adult way. Bringing that out into the open will cause both of you to be ashamed and vulnerable. Only this will create the space to express a heartfelt "I'm sorry," leading to a heartfelt reconnection.

Logosynthesis challenges us to understand phenomena in terms of energy—in our internal and external world. From that energy perspective, forgiveness describes the following process:

- Abe has done something that resulted in Brenda being hurt.

- Energy is frozen in a representation of Abe's behavior in Brenda's energy system. This results in Brenda feeling disappointed, angry or shocked. Brenda thinks Abe's behavior is bad, intolerable, or even "off the wall." This is a *You Make Me Feel* sequence in which Abe is guilty of Brenda feeling bad.

- Something happens that enables Abe to reconnect to Brenda: Abe recognizes that his behavior didn't work out well and excuses himself, or Brenda discovers there were reasons for Abe's behavior, which allows her to change her state of mind.

- The energy bound in the *You Make Me* Feel sequence is released.

AUTONOMY, INDEPENDENCE, RESILIENCE

Everything can be taken from a man but one thing:
the last of the human freedoms—
to choose one's attitude
in any given set of circumstances,
to choose one's own way.

— Viktor Frankl

Autonomy means that the Self rules: In ancient Greek, *autos* means self, *nomos* means a law or a rule. If the Self rules, you're in contact with your purpose, your mission, your contribution to this plane of existence, you're in contact with all of your resources, and you can access and activate your full potential and that of the people around you.

Autonomy is related to independence, interdependence and resilience, but these concepts only address the horizontal dimension of our existence and exclude connection to Essence, the vertical dimension. Autonomy allows for two main characteristics:

▪ Autonomous people feel safe and secure. Because they live in the present, they're able to find security from a deep inner source in themselves. They'll always have access to their own resources and those around them. From that position, they can determine if it's possible to change a situation for the better or if they must accept what is and make the best of it.

▪ Autonomous people learn and develop. They are growing whether circumstances are supportive or adverse. They're able to discover new options in situations where others stick to

Reclaiming Your Energy from Your Emotions **103**

the familiar. That will also give them resilience and immunity against that which destroys others.

Victor Frankl, the founder of Logotherapy, was an impressive example of an autonomous, or resilient, person. In the face of the utter cruelty and despair of the German concentration camps in WWII he managed to stay in contact with his own inner meaning, making him able to offer solace to those surrounding him in an environment of death and destruction.

When I attended two lectures with him in 1994, he was over 90, old and frail. He walked with a cane, and his poor eyesight necessitated someone taking him to the stage. However, as soon as he took the microphone, I was struck by the strength in his voice, and the two thousand people in the room fell silent, filled with awe. He not only spoke but personified meaning: He exemplified living one's mission.

Logos doesn't only mean word, but it also signifies meaning, and that's why Frankl called his school of thought logotherapy. Therefore, the *logo* in Logosynthesis also pays tribute to his work and character.

The synthesis refers to Roberto Assagioli's psychosynthesis.*
Assagioli agreed with Freud that healing childhood trauma and developing a healthy ego were necessary aims of psychotherapy but believed that a personal growth went beyond this. A student of philosophical and spiritual traditions of both East and West, Assagioli sought to address personal growth beyond the norm of the well-functioning ego. He also championed the blossoming of human potential into the spiritual or transpersonal dimensions of human experience.

Standing on the shoulders of these two giants in our work in Logosynthesis, we're trying to clear a space in which the autonomy of your Self and your clients' may unfold, step by step.

*URL: https://en.wikipedia.org/wiki/Psychosynthesis 23.12.2019.

ASTONISHMENT, SURPRISE

Curiosity wants to go this way, that way.
Wondering deepens what is.

— Ludwig Hasler

In astonishment and surprise, your frame of reference opens to new information: You were unaware life could be like this.

If the new information has a negative charge, the astonishment is tinged with disappointment. Broken expectations bring you into contact with the limits of the here-and-now. Your self-confidence may be affected by this disappointment, you may be taken aback. You may need a round of the Logosynthesis sentences to identify your expectations and bridge the gap to the present.

If the new information has a positive charge, it will open doors that were previously closed. In love or in life's purpose, there is connection to awe and respect in the face of life's all-encompassing intensity. You're reconnecting to Essence. There's no need for any further intervention: You just are with *All That Is*.

AWE, RESPECT,
HUMILITY

To see a World in a Grain of Sand
And a Heaven in a Wild Flower,
Hold Infinity in the palm of your hand
And Eternity in an hour.

— William Blake, Auguries of Innocence

When you're in contact with Essence, feelings of awe and respect arise when confronted with the full extent of its power. You may recognize Essence in different ways:

- In your Self, when you have felt guided through challenging times, bringing you nearer to your reason for living.

- In others, when they're acting with compassion, creativity and intelligence, in the service of what they're perceiving as their mission.

- In mystic moments, you experience the overwhelming power of Essence. If you become aware of the full scope of its existence—and your own—you may feel at the same time powerful, humble and grateful to be alive.

However, humility can also be a form of second order dissociation. To avoid abandonment, you have adapted to strong introjects from others. This form of humility blocks your personal and spiritual development. Caught in a repeating pattern of restraining your power in the presence of an authority, you're a humble servant with no purpose of your own.

You gave away your power out of fear: a fear of being rejected, of being left alone. You discovered that others would protect you if you let them take center stage. You must learn to give up this adaptation, and for this, you must experience and trust that the pain of abandonment can be overcome by reconnecting to Essence. This way is better than by adapting to those with worldly power.

At heart, your life is a quest for the awesome—the literal awe you feel when you first grasp something profound. It's a state we all are born with, and you can see it in every child as they discover the world. Awe is often lost as we grow up, as mundane concerns take over our lives. You learn to suppress awe out of a fear of appearing naïve.

In that existential awe, you're recognizing that you're embedded in a Being that's holding you. You're fully aware of your limits, and at the same time you're aware of the tremendous mystery of Essence. You respect this with a humility that mirrors this grand reality. However, you can be humble without losing your own power, because you're aware that you are a spark of that Divine, a cell within the Master's Body.

With the help of Logosynthesis you can accomplish this, step by step, but you may need a strong therapeutic alliance to support you while you explore.

HOPE,
COMMITMENT

The moment one definitely commits oneself,
then providence moves too.
All sorts of things occur to help one that would never otherwise
have occurred.

— John Anster

If you're in dire straits, hope is a state where you desire or wish that something better, more positive, will happen to you in the future. When we look at hope through the lens of Logosynthesis, it's important to consider if the energy in wishes is bound up or flowing freely:

■ If energy is bound in a wish or desire, you're not in contact with the power of your Essence, and you don't access and activate the resources and potential of your Selfg. Instead, you expect some invisible power or authority to step in and improve your situation, and the only thing you can do is wait. Since your energy is bound, separate from your free Self, your hope is futile, and time passes by without change or development. The problem with this kind of hope is that the person doesn't recognize that it keeps them stuck.

■ In constructive hope, you remain in contact with your Essence's intention. You know what you're here for and you trust in your Self and your environment. From this attitude of trust, you're aware that the Universe is Love, and if you connect to this Love from within, everything that happens will have meaning.

As long as your energy is bound, you may need help from a friend or guide in exploring your situation. In this process you identify the fantasy behind the hope in great detail. Only then will you be able to resolve it, release your Self from passivity and commit to your task. After that, all your resources in the here and now are available to improve your life.

Working with Logosynthesis, in self-coaching or with the help of a trained guide, can assist you in ending futile wishing and moving into hope based on trust.

LOVE
WITH A BIG L

Love is the greatest state of all. Love is your connection to Essence. Essence is Love with a capital L. In contact with Love, you experience a continuous flow of life energy, without pain, sorrow, irritation or impatience.

You're in the moment, and you're trusting what the future will bring without any need to control it. The past is gone, you've made it through, and you learned from it what you needed to learn. There is no cause for resentment, regret or grief; you know you did what you could and the same holds true for others.

Now you're connected with Essence, as well as with the world around you. You are aware of your mission, your ultimate purpose, and you know it's a mission for and in the world. In Love, your body and mind are serving your Self, and you're wonderfully in tune with what life is offering in each moment. The needs of your body and mind are less immediate.

Many have this experience when falling in love, in a state of bliss, for weeks, months or even years. In time, dissociative patterns take over, driven by the needs of your body, your mind, your family or your work. If you fall in love, it opens a window to Essence. You realize that there is more to life and you don't need to spend your time building and living out patterns in order to avoid archaic pain and trauma.

Being in love pulls you beyond your familiar patterns, the laws of nature and culture, and that makes it a very precious state. At the same time, you're more your Self than ever and closer to another than you have ever been. Every man or woman who has ever loved has experienced forms of connection that can't be explained by the laws of physics.

The curious absence of patterns fills you with the hope that pain and loneliness are over. You're about to explore a completely new world in which your needs are met: There is a person who notices, accepts and meets them, and it's easy for you to do the same in return.

You're also aware of how fragile this state is, how it can lose its big L and turn into pain and abandonment in a heartbeat. Often, there is a deep fear just below the surface of your consciousness: a fear that this is a dream, joined to a fear that you will make a mistake and drive the other person away.

Falling in love leads to disappointment, anger and even hate if it's rooted in biology and psychology. Based on the spoken or implied expectation that your beloved exists to meet your needs in exchange for you meeting his or her needs. In the long run this expectation, this fantasy, will undermine every new relationship as it creates frozen patterns or reactivates the old ones.

After a while the bliss lessens. What felt endless and exciting fades like a photo of a long-ago holiday. The window to Essence is closed. You know it was open, you remember the bliss, but it's over and a familiar loneliness nags at your joy and confidence.

This can begin a new cycle of looking for love, or it can lead to resentment, rejection, frustration and passivity. Or it can be the beginning of a new stage in your life if you realize it's not the other who is Essence: It is your Self. You didn't look through a window: You were looking in a mirror. You saw your own divine nature reflected in the eyes of the person you loved, but you weren't ready to see it as you. The illusion was that someone lifted the burden of loneliness from your shoulders. In reality, you saw who you are without that load.

Once you realize the truth, processing these archaic wounds is your homework. Look in the mirror and see who you really are with the power of Essence, look at the pain from the past or fear for the future. Logosynthesis can help you identify every aspect of the small and big traumas: the introjects, the fantasies, the transference and the projections. After identifying them, you can localize the triggers of the pain in the space around you and dissolve them.

This creates an open space for Love in your life, and Love will be happy to move in and stay.

BLISS

For reasons I cannot explain
There's some part of me wants to see Graceland
And I may be obliged to defend
Every love, every ending
Or maybe there's no obligations now
Maybe I've a reason to believe
We all will be received in Graceland.

— Paul Simon, Graceland

This time is different. You've never been here before. Your physical structure has given out on you. This is not relaxation: It's surrender. Your muscles tell you, *"You're taken care of."*

At the same time, you move with ever increasing speed into the Light of a thousand suns. The words of the Ascended Masters sound suddenly familiar, until your mind fades as your muscles did. You don't need to think, understand, or control. You're safe.

There are angels. Not the winged characters in white, but beings of radiant light. You know they're similar, but ahead of you: They left their bodies and minds long ago, the bodies and minds humans desperately cling to because they think they can't live without them. These angels are well-versed in the state you've only just entered. A state which you knew existed, and have been seeking for many years, a state for which you have left the familiar. They've been where you are, they know you, and you understand they are what you're becoming. Now they move around easily, and communicate through direct channels, without language as you know it. They're at home, a form of togetherness you haven't felt before.

Your journey goes even further towards the Light. The deeper you go, the more you realize that there is more, even More. You recognize the angels' message to the prophets, about Him, or maybe it's Her. The angels told the prophets what you really are, what we really are, and More. The prophets spoke, inspired our world, even though that world could only grasp single sparks of the Light. You've been reading the words of the prophets all your life, longing for the world of angels. Now you're there and discover that the Light is there, and More.

In this blinding Light, in this warm soft shell that fits you like a glove, you realize that you're a cell. A cell in an endless-ly expanding body. A cell connecting to every other, co-creat-ing a Whole that's greater than the sum of its parts. There is More, so much More.

You remain in this state for what seems like an eternity. Following your body and mind, time has ceased to exist. You just are. The only thing that reminds you of your physicality are the tears. Tears of joy and gratitude for being allowed to be here, to be.

The experience of eternity doesn't last. Your body and mind fatigue in the intensity of the Light. They are not built to re-main here. Slowly, you return to everyday consciousness, with the memory that there is More. A memory that has changed you. Forever.

Remember to always be yourself.
Unless you can be Batman.
Then always be Batman.
— Andy Biersack

The book was almost finished, and I shared an image of the cover design in my Logosynthesis group on Facebook. I was fine with the title and the first subtitle, but the second subtitle: "Stories from Real Life" felt flat, and I asked the group for help. The first ideas that came up didn't appeal to me, but then Karen wrote: "Being yourself." I let her suggestion sink in and decided that the imperative would fit better: "Be Your Self," with the big S we're using in Logosynthesis.

In the background Graham Nash's album "Songs for Beginners" was playing. When I started to change the subtitle in the manuscript, the universe struck me with awe: In the second I typed the words "Be Your Self," the chorus in track 5 sounded from the speakers, softly:

[Chorus]

Be yourself

Be yourself

Free yourself

Free yourself

See yourself

See yourself

Then you can free yourself

Be yourself

Be yourself.

I now had my subtitle, and you have your reminder.

APPENDIX

This appendix contains a disclaimer, a glossary of terms used in the Logosynthesis model, a description of the Logosynthesis Basic Procedure, a short bio of the authors and useful next steps if you want to know more about Logosynthesis.

DISCLAIMER

The information contained in this book is educational in nature and is provided only as general information. The authors and publisher make no representation or warranties with respect to the accuracy, applicability, fitness, or completeness of the contents of this book. The information presented in this text is not intended to represent that Logosynthesis is used to diagnose, treat, cure, or prevent any disease or psychological disorder. The authors and publisher shall in no event be held liable for any loss or other damages, including but not limited to special, incidental, consequential, or other damages. Emotional material may continue to surface after applying Logosynthesis methods, indicating other issues may need to be addressed. Previously vivid or traumatic memories may fade which could adversely impact your ability to provide detailed legal testimony regarding a traumatic incident. Logosynthesis is not a substitute for medical or psychological treatment.

In order to use Logosynthesis with others, you need to become sufficiently trained and certified as a Practitioner in Logosynthesis®. The authors accept no responsibility or liability whatsoever for the use or misuse of the information contained in this book. Please seek professional advice as appropriate before implementing any protocol or opinion expressed in this book.

Application

The application of Logosynthesis helps to free an individual's life energy that's caught in frozen worlds. A stable working relationship is necessary for this application, as is customary in other models of guided change. The application process consists of three steps:

- The person takes back their own energy that's bound up in an introject or an aspect of an introject to a space in their Selves, which is called the "right place."

- The person removes the energy that other people and objects have left behind in their personal space.

- The person takes their own energy that's bound up in reactions to the introject.

The processing takes place when specific sentences are said. The person or their coach or therapist forms these sentences based on information from two meta-questions. The first two sentences are formed with information from meta-question B. Precise answers to the meta-questions A and B are required for accurate application of the Logosynthesis model.

Basic assumptions

Logosynthesis proceeds from four basic assumptions. These assumptions form the foundation of the method and are the reason for its effectiveness. The point of departure is that we are Essence, i.e. beings beyond time and space.

- The lack of awareness of our true nature and task in this world leads to suffering.

■ The awareness of our true nature is reduced or hindered by introjection and dissociation (splitting off.)

■ Split-off parts and introjects are frozen energy structures in multi-dimensional space—not just theoretical concepts.

■ The power of word makes possible the resolution of frozen structures and frees our life energy for our mission.

Belief, Limiting belief

A (limiting) belief hinders one's self-perception and available options in the current environment. It also hinders the unfolding of one's potential. A (limiting) belief can be acquired from important primary relationships—or it can be a conclusion that's reached in reaction to statements made or behaviors demonstrated by these important people.

Black hole

The black hole is the most intense experience of first order dissociation. An individual's contact with Essence and other people is completely cut off and he literally experiences himself as being in a "black hole." The black hole is described in mysticism as "the long dark night of the soul." Neither Essence nor other people are perceived in this state.

Cycle

A sequence of three Logosynthesis sentences with their working pauses. A reflection phase follows a cycle—allowing the processed aspect to be integrated into the client's frame of reference. A session will sometimes contain only one cycle or even no cycles at all, but sessions with between five and seven cycles are not uncommon.

Dissociation

An individual can split off parts—or dissociate—when they're unable to assimilate a trauma or distressing event because it overwhelms their capabilities or development. Their physical, emotional, and cognitive reaction to the trauma or event split off from the flow of life energy, from Essence, and are stored as frozen parts. A representation of the trauma or event is stored as an introject along with the individual's energy or energy from the outside world. Dissociated parts can be activated at any time through similar traumas or events and then lead to similar reactions.

Earth Life System

The Earth Life System is a three-dimensional environment in time that the Self, manifested from Essence, shares with other beings. The Earth Life System contains all the elements of experience that the Self requires to fulfill its task within this environment.

Emotions

Emotions are innate elements of human experience that are directly tied to an individual's perception of his environment and his corresponding accommodation behaviors (e.g. surprise, joy, rage, fear, revulsion, grief).[1] Emotions serve the survival of individuals and social systems by supporting decision-making, the development of values and norms, and the finding of adequate behaviors for interaction with the environment.

Healthy emotions relate to other people or events in the present. Archaic emotions are frozen reactions to people or events

[1] Plutchik, Robert (1980), Emotion: Theory, research, and experience: Vol. 1. Theories of emotion, 1, New York: Academic.

in the past. Logosynthesis acts to identify archaic emotions and to dissolve them, allowing individuals to react with healthy emotions.

Energy structure, pattern
The flow of energy can be influenced by distressing events and then frozen in structures or patterns. These structures contain perceptions that are stored in an individual's body and personal space. They also contain physical, emotional, and cognitive reactions to the perceptions.

Essence
A human being is a manifestation of a comprehensive Essence that exists beyond time and space. Religious and spiritual traditions call Essence the higher Self, the true Self, or the immortal soul. Logosynthesis borrows the term "Essence" from Ali Hameed Almaas and uses it as a neutral concept so as to avoid associations with existing religions, spiritual paths, or schools of guided change. Essence manifests as a Self with a body and psyche in the Earth Life System.

Fantasy
A fantasy is an idea about how the world is, how it could/ should be, or how it could/should have been. It's distinguished from sensory perceptions and memories, both of which represent the world in the past or present with the help of the senses. Fantasies are generally just as important as sensory perceptions and memories. The reality content of fantasies varies; a plan may include concrete steps to bring about its realization, while a wish or dream delegates the realization to other people or elements of the outside world.

Feeling

A feeling can denote an emotion, a fantasy, an intuition, a physical sensation, a kinesthetic perception, a thought, a hypothesis, or a belief. Clarification is always required when this word is used in Logosynthesis, as different meanings can lead to different interventions. Professionals may find it worthwhile to go over the different meanings with their clients.

Foreign energy, non-me energy

Foreign energy is the energy of other people, animals, or objects found in an individual's body or personal space as part of an introject. Foreign energy can lead to frozen reactions and is removed with the aid of the second Logosynthesis sentence.

Frozen perception

A frozen perception is a portion of a frozen world in which the sensory experiences of a memory are frozen into an energetic structure. Frozen perceptions are inseparably linked to frozen reactions. Frozen perceptions are identified with the help of meta-question B and form the topic of the first two Logosynthesis sentences.

Frozen reaction

A frozen reaction is a portion of a frozen world that includes physical, emotional, cognitive, and behavioral aspects. Frozen reactions are always connected to a trigger. The same reactions will always occur if the associated trigger is activated. Logosynthesis is only concerned with reactions that directly or indirectly lead to suffering. These reactions are identified with the help of meta-question A. The problems that clients bring into counselling sessions are generally brought about by frozen reactions.

Frozen world

Introjects are embedded in frozen perceptions of circumstances. Taken together, these form a frozen world. The concept of a frozen world is closely related to Kernberg's object relations in psychological terms, i.e. an image of a primary relationship is inseparable from a certain emotional state. Kernberg's model fails to include energetic components, however. Our life energy is generally bound up in frozen worlds to a significant extent, and it's these frozen worlds that determine our reaction patterns and form our identities.

Introjection

Events can't be processed if they go beyond the scope of an individual's existing frame of reference and the individual receives no support in processing the event. Representations of people and events then become introjects. Introjects contain energy taken from the individual's Self as well as energy from other people or objects that's been left in the individual's personal space.

Introjects, Activation of

Frozen worlds help us to orient ourselves in life; they create stability in our perceptions of ourselves in our environments. Activated introjects explain much of our daily emotions, thoughts, and actions. When an event causes a painful reaction, however, its introject may also be activated in the future and lead to similar painful reactions. The affected individual is only able to trace these reactions in a limited manner. Logosynthesis is applied when an individual suffers because pain-generating introjects are activated on a daily basis and the individual's normal life in society is inhibited as a result.

Life energy

Life energy is the power of growth within nature that causes organisms to develop into higher forms, embryos to become adults, and healthy people to strive after their ideals. This power has different names in various cultures, including ka, physis, prana, chi, the zero point field, and, in this book, Essence. Life energy can be flowing or frozen and can belong to an individual or to people and objects within an individual's environment.

Personal space

An individual's personal space is a part of the 3-dimensional field in the Earth Life System that the individual experiences as his own. Personal space usually contains the individual's physical body as well as introjects and dissociated parts. A personal space can equally be understood as an extended aura or an energy field.

Processing

The Logosynthesis sentences have been developed for and are addressed to elements of experience such as memories and fantasies. The saying of each sentence is followed by a working pause in which the power of the word neutralizes or assimilates the targeted element. Once a sentence's processing is complete, the emotional charge of the targeted element is reduced or has disappeared. The individual can then gauge the experience from an age-appropriate perspective. Traumatic memories lose their potential to cause anxiety or pain in the wake of processing; the individual can now perceive the traumatic events in a proper context.

Representation

A representation, or image, is a three-dimensional energy structure in space that's formed of frozen sensory perceptions (i.e. sight, hearing, touch, smell, taste.) It can depict a memory, fantasy, or belief. Representations (or images) must be assimilated to become functional.

Self

The Self is a specific manifestation of Essence with a dedicated purpose within the context of the Earth Life System. The Self controls a body with which it perceives the environment and navigates space—along with a brain that processes information from the sensory organs. It also controls a psyche that directs the body and brain in their confrontations with the environment.

Parts of the energy of the Self can be split off, frozen or dissociated. The part of the Self in which a person's life energy is flowing freely is called the free Self.

Sentences

See Logosynthesis in a Nutshell.

Subjective Units of Distress (SUDs)

SUDs are a measurement of the level of distress a person is experiencing on a scale from 0 to 10. Zero means absolutely no distress, 10 is the maximum level. We don't do 11 or 100, even though people sometimes give such an answer. The concept was developed by Joseph Wolpe in 1969.* It's has been used in the treatment of anxiety disorders since.

Trauma

A trauma is the consequence of a distressing event that an individual is unable to process. Logosynthesis considers a trauma to consist of a strong connection of frozen perceptions and ideas with physical, emotional, cognitive, and behavioral reactions. A trauma is dissolved through the application of the Logosynthesis sentences to the frozen perceptions and ideas—causing the reactions to disappear.

Trigger

A trigger is an energy pattern that's activated by people or events in an individual's current environment. Triggers are based on frozen perceptual patterns associated with memories, fantasies and beliefs. They inevitably lead to predictable physical, emotional, and cognitive reactions.

Working pause

See Logosynthesis in a Nutshell.

*Wolpe, Joseph (1969). The Practice of Behavior Therapy, New York: Pergamon Press..

LOGOSYNTHESIS
IN A NUTSHELL

If you are familiar with Logosynthesis, you'll know its application always follows a similar path:

- First, you build a solid working alliance with the person in front of you. You must reach a level of trust necessary for a person to leave their comfort zone on a trip into unknown territory. Your clients must know they're in good hands and be confident that the tools and techniques you use will help them on their life path. They're not questioning your methods: they trust you in the way they trust their family dentist or their car mechanic.

- Once your client feels welcomed, you start to explore the reasons why they have come to you and create a space to let them open up and tell their story. This is a precious moment for many people; they meet you in moments of suffering and tend to feel profound relief when someone is really listening.

- As they tell the story, you start to listen for cues that can guide your work into the next stage. How does the client describe the world they live in? How big are the power and influences they experience? Are they able to think clearly, or are they caught in memories, fantasies and beliefs?

- Which emotions show up, and how do these guide your client's behavior?

- Once the client has begun to feel comfortable with the setting and with you as a guide, you can start to explore what is behind the world as the client perceives it. What is triggering the emotions and physical sensations the client is feeling? What is in the present, what is hidden in history? What are their fantasies about the future? You carefully direct the client from the presented issue to a world that has not yet been explored.

■ Now you find the level of distress the client is experiencing regarding the presented issue, and you move from listening to the story as a whole to exploring essential aspects: Which people, times, and places were significant in the creation of this distress? Many complaints that appear firmly related to the present are in fact deeply rooted in painful events of the past.

■ When you have found out what is triggering the client to feel as they feel, you start designing the Logosynthesis sentences for the trigger of the unpleasant experiences. You only offer those sentences if the client has reached a receptive stage in which they are open to you and to all the methods you will want to use to resolve their issues. This openness is located between dependency and resistance: If a client depends entirely on you, they are probably reluctant to take responsibility themselves, and if they're resistant, they won't allow the sentences to work as designed.

■ Each sentence contains a label X, which stands for the frozen perception of a memory, a fantasy or a belief. As a rule, that means you're able to see, hear, sense, smell or taste X.

■ X never contains an emotion or a reaction to a perception. For many professionals, this is somewhat unusual, because traditional schools of guided change tend to focus more on emotional reactions than on the perception of the events that trigger those emotions.

■ Before you continue, have a glass of water ready. Often a client feels tired, dizzy or nauseous. These signs indicate intense processing and usually disappear when the client drinks water.

■ When the client is ready for a step into the unknown, you offer them the first sentence and ask them to repeat it.

■ You provide each sentence in small chunks—this is not a memory exercise—you let the client repeat that part and take the time to let each sentence sink in. In time you'll recognize the signs that the sentence has finished processing and offer the next one.

■ The first sentence is:

I retrieve all my energy, bound up in (this perception)
X and take it to the right place in my Self.

You say that sentence in parts, and you invite the client to repeat each part after you. In the beginning, this may be unfamiliar, but in fact, it's not much different from a family doctor asking a patient to say "Ah."

■ After the client has repeated a sentence, you offer a working pause to process the information that has been given to their system through the sentence. In this pause, different reactions are possible, from yawning and relaxation to deep emotions. If emotions show up, let the client repeat the sentence without interrupting the cycle with discussion.

- The same procedure is applied to the second sentence:

I remove all non-me energy, related to (this perception) X, from all of my cells, all of my body and my personal space, and send it to where it truly belongs.

Again, followed by a working pause.

- The third sentence follows the same pattern, again with a working pause:

I retrieve all my energy, bound up in all my reactions to (this perception) X and take it to the right place in my Self.

- After the series of three sentences and their working pauses, you create a space for the experience, and invite the client to share their process, usually with the help of an open-ended question, such as "What's happening now?" This will reveal if the current issue has been resolved or if additional exploration and processing is needed.

- If the level of distress has been sufficiently reduced and nothing new comes up, the next step of the process is *future pacing*: You invite the client to imagine the future in order to determine if the experienced distress has completely disappeared. If this is not the case, begin a new cycle, focusing on the issue that showed up in the future pacing.

- If everything is resolved and future pacing no longer causes distress, you can close the cycle and explore what else needs to be done in the session.

- The more you use Logosynthesis, on your own issues or

with clients, the easier it becomes to apply the standard protocol of Logosynthesis, the Basic Procedure. There are endless variations possible, but they can all be reduced to these steps.

■ For many trainees and Practitioners, it is a continuous challenge to let go of preexisting skills and knowledge of coaching, counseling and psychotherapy. In Logosynthesis it is often unnecessary to linger with intense emotions: The search for the trigger of these emotions and its neutralization will bring faster relief than the most empathic form of staying with them.

■ It is also unnecessary to interpret events or offer a new frame of reference to help a client understand what is happening in their life or how to enact change. As soon as the power of words has done its work, many clients are well equipped to come to this new understanding themselves, to their surprise and to mine.

■ Working with Logosynthesis is often about thinking less and doing less. I tend to say: "As a Practitioner in Logosynthesis you must be lazy, stupid and slow." You don't need much effort, because the words themselves will do the work. You don't need to think or interpret on behalf of the client, because the client will gain their own mental clarity in the course of the process. You don't need any speed in your interventions, on the contrary: You can sit on your hands until the processing pause has ended, and the client reconnects with you.

ABOUT THE AUTHORS

Dr. Willem Lammers

Dr. Lammers is a Swiss psychologist, psychotherapist, coach and consultant to organizations with 40+ years of experience in the field.

Trained in Transactional Analysis, Gestalt therapy, hypnotherapy, NLP and various energy psychology modalities, he has held positions at a university and in a hospital. In 1992, he became self-employed and founded his own institute for professional training in psychotherapy, coaching, supervision and organizational development.

While searching for a more elegant, effective and direct way to guide people through pain, to realize their potential, he became increasingly aware that we are more than our physical body and our mind. In 2005, he discovered Logosynthesis® and now trains professionals in this new, simple but effective model for self-coaching, counselling and psychotherapy.

In 2014, Willem co-founded the Logosynthesis International Association, which is now responsible for certifying professionals in Logosynthesis as both practitioners and trainers of this elegant method for guided change.

In 2018, Dr. Lammers received the prestigious ACEP Award for his major contribution to the field of energy psychology. His work has been translated into German, Italian, Dutch, Serbian and English. This is his tenth book.

Dr. Lammers lectures and teaches internationally. He also offers online courses and frequently participates in various

Logosynthesis discussion groups on social media. His teaching schedule and additional resources can be found at The Origin of Logosynthesis®, his training institute.

Website: http://www.logosynthesis.net/

Email: info@logosynthesis.net

Lara Cardona Morisset, M.Ed

Lara Cardona Morisset is a coach and educational specialist at bloom, an online resource for coaching and Logosynthesis based in Los Angeles. As a certified Practitioner and Instructor in Logosynthesis®, she specializes in working with creatives.

Lara holds a Master of Education and has over a decade of teaching experience. She began using Logosynthesis as a method of self-coaching to transform every aspect of her life, and now enjoys a profession guiding others to do the same.

Lara offers online workshops in using Logosynthesis for self-coaching, and individual Logosynthesis sessions. A variety of applications of Logosynthesis can be found on her YouTube channel. Just google her name on YouTube.

Website: www.bloom-think.com

Email: lara@bloom-think.com

OTHER BOOK TITLES BY DR. WILLEM LAMMERS

■ Lammers, Willem (2001). *The Energy Odyssey. New Directions in Energy Psychology.* Maienfeld, Switzerland: ias.

■ Lammers, Willem (2006). *Chefsache. Essays für Coaches und Manager/innen.* Chur, Switzerland: Desertina.

■ Lammers, Willem (2008). *Logosynthesis. Change through the Magic of Words.* Maienfeld, Switzerland: ias. Also in German.

■ Lammers, Willem (2009). *Phrases to Freedom. Self-Coaching with Logosynthesis.*

■ Lammers, Willem (2015). *Self-Coaching with Logosynthesis.* Also available in German, Serbian and Italian.

■ Lammers, Willem (2015). *Logosynthesis Handbook for the Helping Professions.* Also in German and Dutch.

■ Lammers, Willem (2019). *Minute Miracles. The Practice of Logosynthesis. Inspiration from Real Life.* Also available in German.

■ Weiss Laurie and Lammers, Willem (2020). *Embrace Prosperity. Resolve Blocks to Experiencing Abundance. Rapid Relief with Logosynthesis.*

All books are available through most online book retailers.

LIA, THE INTERNATIONAL ASSOCIATION

The Logosynthesis International Association (LIA) is an independent, international non-profit organisation based in Switzerland. It was founded in March 2014 and serves the continuous development of Logosynthesis as well as the distribution, quality management and acceptance of the model. The LIA develops criteria for the structure and content of training programs and certifies Practitioners, Instructors, Master Practitioners and Trainers in Logosynthesis.

LIA:
- supports professionals and other interested parties with Logosynthesis
- establishes a worldwide Logosynthesis network with numerous active hubs
- offers a platform for the exchange of knowledge and experience
- contributes to the spreading of Logosynthesis
- promotes the quality and further development of Logosynthesis
- certifies professionals across various levels.

LIA members are trained specialists from counselling, educational and medical professions.

www.logosynthesis.international

Made in the USA
Monee, IL
23 September 2023

43260846R00077